ROBERT SMITH ('NIGE')

A
DOCKYARD
APPRENTICE'S STORY

A DOCKYARD
APPRENTICE'S STORY

MEMOIRS
Cirencester

Published by Memoirs

MEMOIRS
PUBLISHING

25 Market Place, Cirencester, Gloucestershire, GL7 2NX
info@memoirsbooks.co.uk www.memoirspublishing.com

Printed in England

CONTENTS

I dedicate this little book to my parents:

My dad, who like all other dads, just wanted the best for his son.

My dear old mum, who spent half her life trying to
get me out of bed to go to work.

FOREWORD

To enter Chatham Dockyard as an apprentice you took an entrance examination, then chose your preferred trade at an induction day. The highest qualified in the examination made their choices progressively until all the vacancies were filled.

Often electrical engineering apprenticeships were the first to be taken, followed by mechanical fitters, shipwrights, shipfitters, coppersmiths, boilermaker, patternmakers, carpenters, painters and so on.

When I entered the dockyard in 1958, there were approximately 6000 people employed on a site stretching about two miles in length and enclosing hundreds of workshops, offices and storehouses. At this time it had a dedicated police establishment, a fire service, a medical centre, a technical college, a telephone exchange, three main (and several mobile) canteens and dedicated training facilities.

There were also three large ship-refitting basins, eight main docks, various slipways and a very large (60 ton) floating crane. A nuclear submarine refitting facility was operational from 1968 onwards, capable of '2 stream' nuclear refuelling.

Many local engineering firms in the Medway Towns benefited from the training and skills pool of the dockyard, such as Berry Wiggins, Blaw Knox, Wingets, CAV and Elliots. Likewise many local suppliers were badly affected when the dockyard effectively closed in 1985 - for example suppliers of tools, metals, fastenings, paint and building supplies, as well as training establishments. The impact of the dockyard's closure is still apparent in the Medway Towns.

YEAR ONE: APPRENTICES' TRAINING CENTRE

'Oi, get off that bloody bike!' Such was my introduction to the MoD in general and Chatham Dockyard in particular. It was my first day at work, Monday September 22 1958, and I had just cycled the four miles or so from my home in Rainham, Kent, to the dockyard at Chatham.

I had already done a 'recce' so that I would know where the point of entry (Pembroke Gate) into the dockyard would be, but no one had bothered to explain that you had to get off your bike and WALK through the gate entrance. The copper who shouted the order was one of the biggest blokes I had ever seen, more so as he was wearing a full-length black uniform raincoat. It was about ten to seven, and although only late September, with a strong wind and driving rain it felt more like midwinter. He looked cold, wet, and fed up and looked as if he wanted me to know about it.

He gave me my first dockyard bollocking in a broad Scottish accent, such that I could only guess at about every third word. However, after a couple of heated minutes he did explain to me where within the 'yard I was expected to go for my induction.

The Apprentices' Training Centre (ATC) was on the south side of the engineering factory and just to the north side of the chain test house. It consisted of two parallel single-storey brick buildings, connected by an internal passageway with a corrugated asbestos roof.

The two wings were mirror image workshops and in the centre was the main entrance with clocking on/off area, instructors' offices and toilets, apprentices' toilets and a lecture room at the back. The workshop areas had two long banks of metal-topped workbenches, with a vice and a drawer every five feet or so, and at the end of the workshop was a small pillar drill. The whole facility was illuminated by bright fluorescent lighting. This was to be my home for the next 12 months.

On arrival at the ATC we were mustered together and met by our instructors, who introduced themselves as Mr Eddie Turner and Mr Joe Ward. Eddie was a big man, above average height and stocky. He had a black moustache and glasses and was balding. Joe was also tall, thinner and even more bald. Our names were checked against the entry list and we were given the following information:

- We would clock on and off in the entrance to this building, and our hours of work would be Monday–Thursday, 0700 - 1700hrs. (One hour lunch break between 1200-1300) and Friday 0700–1600. That was a 44-hour week.

- We would be paid (a subject of great interest to us!) on Friday lunchtime at 1200, but not this first week as we had to work a week in hand.

- Our rate of pay would be £2 11s 2d (1s 3d per hour).

- If we were late, ie 'clocked on' one minute late (at 0701), this was considered to be 'absent on parade' and we would be stopped a quarter of an hour's pay. Further lateness or re-occurrences incurred additional penalties, as I was to discover later.

- We would be required to attend the Dockyard Technical College for up to two days' release weekly, to obtain appropriate technical qualifications.

- We would be granted 88 hours' paid leave (two weeks' holiday) per year.

- We would be issued with two sets of coveralls (overalls), one on and one in the wash, and the basic hand tools we would require in learning our hand tool skills.

We were told that we would be trained in this centre for the next 12 months, and during that time we would master the basic skills using hand tools, hacksaws, hammers and chisels, files and scrapers. We would be tested periodically to ensure that we were achieving the standard required by means of 'test jobs'. A test job had to be completed satisfactorily before the next stage of the training could start.

We had all left school, mostly quite thankful to have done so, with fairly high hopes and an optimistic outlook. But that had been in July. Now, several months later, cycling into a headwind to work at 6.15 on a cold October morning to file pieces of steel plate for eight and a half hours a day, it didn't seem such a good deal after all.

Perhaps school wasn't so bad? No, on reflection, in spite of the above, school was worse.

And we were now getting paid! Even if there would be no money for the first week. We would have to work for two weeks before we secured our first pay packets. And we were getting £2 11s 2d! How on earth would we spend all that? The answer was easy: I gave my mum £1 a week for my keep (and often borrowed at least some of it back during the week) and was left with £1 11s 2d, which I promised not to waste.

After a few months we had a pay rise, to £2 13s 0d: look out high rollers, here we come! This didn't seem a lot of money for the hours we worked, especially as some of our mates were working as labourers/teaboys on building sites and getting £5 a week.

We sorted ourselves out and found positions at the workbench that we liked or alongside someone we knew. This seemed quite important, as we were to make this our home for the next 12 months. Each position had a large work-vice fixed to the bench and a big drawer to keep our bits in. The floor alongside the benches was covered with duckboards - wooden slatted floor covers which kept our feet off the cold floor.

Several schoolfriends had started with me, so at least I could recognize some of the faces, which made the whole 'new boy' experience less daunting. From the outset my real name was ignored and I was known as Nige, mainly because several years earlier I had decided that Nige (Nigel) was a far classier name, and would be a distinct advantage to me when trying to impress the opposite sex.

Although we mostly put on a brave face, none of us really knew what to expect, and were suffering more than a little with first-day nerves.

Needless to say, the first few days went very quickly as we all struggled to adapt to our new environment and culture. We were always conscious of the fact that the 'big boys' in the other workshop wing, six months ahead of us in their training, might well be looking for signs of weakness.

So the training started. The principle aim of first-year training was to ensure that we could master basic hand tool skills. We were issued with files: flat, half round, square and triangular. These came in grades, rough, medium and smooth. We were also issued with scrapers (various), chisels (various), a hacksaw, hammer, and measuring equipment (rule and calipers). More elaborate measuring equipment was issued from the stores on an as-required basis. We were encouraged to purchase any additional tools required through the Naval Stores system.

With these basic tools we were required to handcraft metal objects to make them square, flat or regular to very fine limits - thousands of an inch. This would be achieved by practice, practice, and even more practice. (I had a nasty feeling that this was going to be boring, boring, and even more boring.)

At lunchtimes we had the opportunity to investigate a bit

more of the dockyard. After eating our sandwiches, which most of us ate sitting on our toolboxes alongside our workbench, we were free to wander and investigate freely as long as we remembered to clock on again before 1300 hrs.

Incidentally, I made the mistake of saying I enjoyed the cheese sandwiches my mum had packed up for me; consequently I had cheese sandwiches, with slight variations, for the next 10 years. Most of the lads took sandwiches and, like me, a bottle of milk to drink, as we hadn't yet discovered the delights of a good brew, and we certainly couldn't afford the canteen.

At the side of the ATC was a large cycle–rack, mainly for the use of the apprentices, though workmen in the area used it as well. Cycles were still the main transport for most workmen at this time, although a few of the advanced apprentices from the other workshop had motorbikes, which they usually parked outside the main entrance.

At the north end of our workshop, between the workshop and the factory, was a large old-style toilet block. These toilets had a full-length urinal on one side and about 12 cubicles on the other. The toilet doors covered only the middle section, with a gap of about 18 inches at top and bottom so that the chargemen (supervisors) could easily locate and identify any shirkers.

The other unusual design feature of these toilets was that they were 'pre-flush'. The toilet seats were located above a gulley which travelled the full length of the toilet block and was fed with running water. They worked pretty well, apparently, but were an ideal source for 'skylarking' or pranks. One particular morning when all the 'traps' were full, some joker set alight a large bundle of cotton waste and floated it down the flushing gulley. Successive shouts of surprise and obscenities followed the burning waste as it slowly barbequed the bums above. I learned a lot of new words that day!

Unfortunately one of the occupants towards the end of the stream, with the fire well ablaze, was a little slow to react and ended up with a badly-singed scrotum, so there was hell to pay. That particular toilet block was modernized shortly afterwards. Perhaps the culprit had a role to play in the modernization programme.

The nearest workshop to the ATC was the Engineering Factory. This was the largest single building in the dockyard, being approximately 150 yards square. The first entry into this workshop was very impressive. A main gangway went through the centre, wide enough to allow access for large lorries, Lister trucks (the preferred dockyard transport) and a railway track, to accommodate the really large or heavy items. In the central area were located the stores areas at ground level, and offices above. Branching out from the central area were the various sections, which performed multifarious activities.

The submarine section was where the massive diesel engines (Admiralty Standard Range, known as ASRs) were built. These were the main propulsion units in conventional (non-nuclear) submarines at that time. The section also refitted (repaired) other large associated components.

Most of the central factory area was occupied with machine

tool sections, which included heavy turning, light turning, capstan and computer-controlled lathes, milling machines, slotting and shaping machines, grinders and jig borers. Other sections included a valve refitting area, turbine auxiliaries and pumps, water pressure testing, a maintenance section and a toolroom. In the north east corner additional newer offices housed the Inspections area (DDI - delegated dimensional inspection), the Foreman's office on the ground floor, and the Inspectors' offices above.

This workshop had a massive headroom, being similar in height to the Boilershop (which is now part of the Dockside shopping outlet), and it seemed alive with a banging heartbeat; running machinery, overhead crane movements and an acrid smell of oils, paint, and the burning smell of metals being machined which hung over the whole expanse like an unseen envelope.

It was daunting, but very interesting. How on earth did all of these people know what they were doing?

Just walking through this workshop was an education in itself. There were so many men, and although they were all dressed in the issue coveralls, they seemed to be of completely different appearance. There were big strong guys hauling components into place, little fellas, nimble and busy, the moustachioed, the bearded, the bald and the 'cheesecutter' adorned, all equally focused and concentrated.

At every corner were the key men in this panorama, the section labourers, who endlessly swept the factory floor and kept the gangways clear. This then was the Engineering Factory.

The other major workshop in this area, next to the factory, was the Boilershop. When I first walked through this shop, it immediately reminded me of Dante's Inferno. As soon as you entered you heard the THUMP THUMP of the massive hammers forming red-hot workpieces into their required shapes. Then the crackling sound of welding could be heard, along with the bright flashes created, which looked like lightning, while the coarse, acrid fumes attacked the senses. Riveting was still commonplace in the Dockyard at this time and several riveters could be working simultaneously. The noise was unbelievable.

The Boilershop, like many of the other workshops, was split into two separate but complementary sections; the 'main shop' workforce and the 'afloat' gang. The latter were the gang that worked principally on the ships, although they would bring assemblies or components back to the workshop to work on.

I was to discover the dozens of other workshops which made up the dockyard facility in due course, and to learn a little of what the other trades did and how. At this early stage, however, the need to concentrate on my own training, and the limited time away from the training centre, meant that this would have to wait.

It was important to get into a routine. Endless days were spent filing pieces of steel plate. First we had to get a surface flat. The edge of a rule would be held against the filed area and it was held up to the light. If any light could be seen through the join it was unsatisfactory. Eddie Turner had a favorite saying at this stage. He would look at the apprentice offering the work with a condescending frown and say in a very loud voice 'Is it all right? No it's bloody not all right! I could drive a horse and cart through there!' It got so that the whole group could see this coming and would join in, in chorus.

The next stage was to file square. This would be checked with a set square. Once this was mastered the basics had been achieved.

Sometimes additional minor items would be required (eg chalk and emery paper) to polish and finish prepared work. These were loaned out by the instructors, who made us guard them until it was time for their return to the store room. It didn't take us long to find out that we could go to the factory next door and get these items by the handful - which we did.

One day Dick Seamark, a real joker, had a slight accident and tore his coveralls. When it was time for him to hand them in for replacement, Eddie Turner went ballistic. 'This is malicious damage, and you could well be charged with a criminal offence!' he roared. He went on and on and really laid into the lad. Dick was so terrified he shat himself. Although none of us really believed he was going to be shot at dawn, it left us with a feeling of unease. What could happen to us?

It was completely unnecessary for Eddie to get his pleasure like that. The rest of the lads looking on were quite concerned, but we could not believe that this incident was worth all the aggro. Of course, once we all discovered that the bollocking was unnecessary and that the instructors in reality had no teeth at all, it was payback time. And it didn't take long.

Our craft training was supplemented by regular technical lectures. These could be hard work, as the topics, such as case hardening of steels, were not always of paramount interest to a group of sixteen year olds. But there was another problem. Both instructors tried their best, but neither had even a modicum of instructional technique. Eddie in particular had a slight speech impediment (a stutter) and difficulty with long words.

The day to remember started fairly normally. The subject was metallurgy, and specifically the elements which can be added to steels to harden them. Eddie wasn't having a good day and was struggling quite early on with some of the compounds. When he stumbled and stuttered he became flustered, and when he became flustered he stuttered.

His lecture should have gone along the lines of 'Various elements can be added to steels to change their characteristics or to harden them; often used for this purpose is molybdenum, likewise chromium'. Unfortunately Eddie's problem with some of the longer words or technical descriptions had raised its ugly head and on this particular day he struggled. 'Molib… molub… molob… melobdenum…' he stuttered. By now a titter had risen among the gathered apprentices. As Eddie got more and more flustered, a cacophony of laughter shook the room.

Eddie went into a scarlet rage. 'Stop laughing! Stop, STOP!' he shouted. This only made things worse. By now most of us were barely remaining continent.

In exasperation Eddie glowered at the helpless mass in front of him and shouted 'Right, I'll have your tea-stop breaked!' (He meant tea-break stopped, of course).

Utter pandemonium followed. The instructor from the adjacent work area rushed in – I think he imagined it was a bomb scare - to find 25 apprentices paralytic with laughter and a purple-faced instructor, hair standing on end, eyes bulging and neck veins twitching.

By this time we lads had made friends and unconsciously sorted ourselves out into groups of like-minded mates. In fact most of the lads had exactly the same interests - crumpet (girls), pop music and where to go to find both. Some of the lads were natural comedians and kept the rest of us in fits of laughter. Pete Appleby and Dave Riley were particularly funny, with the most original sayings and masterful timing.

I had for my part made friends with Bernard 'Paddy' Hargan, Dave 'Panda' Campbell and Vic Salmon, with whom I shared an interest in motorbikes, as we were both to own the same model of BSA through our apprenticeships.

After the initial settling-in period, when everything was new and strange, the ensuing weeks became less and less interesting, thanks to the repeated and prolonged tasks given to us. These were jobs which necessitated cutting off pieces of material, bar or plate, with a hacksaw and then using files or scrapers to finish and smooth items as shown on engineering drawings or sketches. It soon became very soul-destroying; it was repetitive, monotonous and uninspiring. The problem was exacerbated by the time of year and the cold dark and wet weather. We hardly saw any daylight - talk about battery hens!

The boredom of doing the same tasks every day, filing, filing, and more filing to produce a finished item, created a sense of creeping death.

It was no wonder that some of the lads created amusing situations to relieve the boredom. One such incident occurred when we had a delivery of large metal bar blanks (4' bar, cut approx. 1' thick), the material required in preparation for our next (imminent) test jobs.

Dick Seamark spotted Joe Ward going into the toilet. The instructors had their own toilets, which were padlocked when not in use, but Joe had left the padlock on the outside of the door unlocked. Dick crept up to the door and quietly closed the padlock, trapping Joe inside.

Chuckling like a demented fool, Dick carried a couple of bar blanks over to the toilet and rolled them under the door. An agitated mumbling and swearing could be heard from beyond the door, and people started to enter the toilet to investigate. Dick rolled in more bars and a couple of other lads joined in, until about 12 of these blanks had been forced into the toilet cubicle with Joe. We were in stitches, and the more Joe cussed the funnier it got. He was eventually released by the other instructor.

By now we had started our technical studies at the Dockyard Technical College, which was located in what we called the 'Khyber Pass', just outside the Dockyard. I was started in the National Certificate stream, which meant attending on two days a week (Monday and Thursday).

This was good news and bad. The good news was that it was a later start and took me away from that bloody filing, but the bad news was that it was of course just the same as going back to school again. Most of the lads were not really interested, and we were not sufficiently mature to realize that any qualifications achieved would dramatically improve our career prospects. We were however sufficiently astute to show the necessary level of interest to protect the day's release - well, it was better than work, wasn't it?

I don't recall much about my time at the college, although it lasted for three years in all. The last year was a repeat year, as I had failed to pass the previous year's exam, and I had to apply to repeat the year by way of an interview with the College Principle, Mr Ferguson.

I remember 'Fergie' Ferguson for two reasons. The first was an incident that happened one day when several of us were skylarking in the corridor outside the classrooms. Exit Mr Ferguson, who was not very pleased, and told us so. As we slunk away Paddy mouthed off 'silly old bastard, just because he's past it!' Unfortunately it was just loud enough for Fergie to hear.

I'm sure he caught up with Paddy in two bounds. He spun Paddy round and challenged him in his broad Scots accent by saying 'Past it am I? Put 'em up and let's see how good you are!'

Paddy went to put his mitts up but was thumped so hard on the shoulder, that he staggered back and ended up on his bum, red faced and sheepish. We later found out that in his younger days 'Fergie' had been a very talented amateur boxer.

The second reason was really very sad. I had met Fergie's daughter Pat through one of my ex-girlfriends, Sandra Levene.

Pat struck me as being very friendly and highly intelligent. Tragically, not long afterwards, while out on a hen night, she was killed. The accident happened halfway down the old Bluebell Hill road, a notorious blackspot. Fergie was never the same again.

This is not the whole story though, as this was the accident which triggered off dozens of ghost stories and sightings around the bus stop near the spot where it had happened. There have been so many over such a long period of time that I am convinced there is something unexplained here. Pat, or one of the hen party, appeared on a fairly regular basis, for varying lengths of time and different circumstances, and some of the people who made these contacts were left severely traumatized.

Soon it was time for our first test job, made from the bar steel which had been used to trap Joe in the toilet. This male hexagon, which we had just made, had to be rotated through its six positions, fitting accurately into the female so that no light could be seen through the joints at any of the positions. We all passed fairly easily, although a few of the lads had to do a bit of rework.

When we had our mini-breaks during the day, we would be busy scrounging cigarettes off each other. 'Tailor mades' were a rare commodity (except perhaps the odd packet of Weights on a payday), so invariably this would mean 'roll-ups'. Most of the lads smoked Golden Virginia, Hearts of Oak or Old Holborn, and could roll the ciggies as thin as the matches they lit them with. The tobacco was sold in vending machines outside the main (No. 3) canteen. Golden Virginia was two shillings for half an ounce.

The other main topic of interest during the day was where we were going that night. Usually we would arrange to go to a youth club, as there seemed to be one available most nights of the week and they were cheap. Looking back, perhaps it wasn't cutting-edge entertainment - a game of table tennis, listen to the latest records and a chance to meet a few girls - but it gave us a chance to exaggerate last night's successes, and something to look forward to for the night ahead.

The relationship with our instructors was now on a much more mature level. They were not threatening us with hanging or keelhauling any more and we were showing them the respect that we now realized they deserved.

Eddie Turner was still a problem, in so far as he was extremely prone to exaggeration concerning his wartime exploits. Of course his stories got ever more exaggerated through successive telling by apprentices to other apprentices, the classic being when he supposedly saw a torpedo homing in on the ship he was on. He had jumped overboard, straddled the torpedo and guided it safely passed his ship! The age-old problem, of course, was that as he told these stories over and over again, in the end he started to believe them himself.

The time went past quite quickly. It soon was almost Christmas, and we were all looking forward to our first bank holiday. We had heard that the factory organized some sort of celebration, so a few of us decided that we would go missing for a short while to investigate.

When we entered the factory in mid afternoon the change

that had taken place was impressive. Obviously it was much quieter than usual and there was no banging or loud machinery operating, but most of the sections had put up a few paper chains, tinsel, or some other kind of decoration. As the daylight was already failing, the glimmering bench lights reflecting off the decorations transformed the place. In the central area were large marking out slabs (metal tables), and a crowd was gathering here, all in good humour.

Suddenly there were shouts of 'Keith! Keith!' and clapping. Apparently Keith, one of the workshop labourers, had been encouraged to sing a few carols for us. It should be explained that he had severe learning difficulties. Short and bald, he wasn't a very commanding figure. Although it started as a 'piss-take', when this lost soul stood up on the table and sang *Silent Night* (very badly), the mood gradually changed, and most of us had lumps in our throats.

Getting to work in the winter months wasn't much fun. It might be useful here to explain that things were a lot different in those days. My home was not in a neglected state or even in a 'poor' neighbourhood, but we did not have the luxuries that we take for granted now.

We lived in a three-bedroom semi- detached house which had been privately built but acquired by the Council when the builder got into difficulties. It had two rooms plus a kitchen downstairs, and through the kitchen a ground-floor rear extension housed the toilet and coal store.

We had no central heating, double glazing, fitted carpets or inside toilet. Upstairs consisted of two main bedrooms, a 'box' bedroom, and a bathroom. The two main bedrooms had open fire grates, which were never used, as they were too small to be effective and the coal that was available was of extremely poor quality. The amount of smoke and ash generated, plus the need to empty and re-lay the fire each morning, made them impracticable. Only once, when my Dad was ill in bed, did I ever see these fires used as a last resort. We quite rightly considered them to be dangerous.

Neither my box bedroom nor the bathroom had electric lighting. Both had ceiling-mounted, blanked-off gas fittings (thank goodness that they were blanked off!) Presumably at the time of building gas lighting was envisaged.

The bathroom contained a bath, a wash basin and a boiling copper (which was used to heat the bath water). There was no hot water supply, and no upstairs toilet.

I mention the above to show that it was a real challenge on cold winter mornings to get out of bed, put your feet on to ice-cold linoleum and quickly dress while freezing cold. A quick slosh of cold water in the bathroom was usually a trial, and most mornings ice would form on the inside of the bathroom window. It was bloody cold.

I had started off cycling to work on my rather nice racing bike, a Rotrax: it had a lightweight frame and alloy wheels, the whole business. The problem was that the dockyard roads were not suitable for such a bike. Apart from the potholes, most roads had at least one set of railway lines, more often than not several, and hitting these at any speed usually meant that you ended up on the ground and the bike would be damaged. So it was time for a change, and reluctantly I sold the Rotrax and bought a Triumph of a more heavy-duty nature on HP.

There was a slight gap between selling and getting the new bike, which meant I had to get the bus. The bus journey was a nightmare; it had to be endured to be believed. The bus left Rainham about 6.30 and seemed to be stopping every 100 yards or so. It took forever to get to the dockyard. The bus was almost full by the time I got on, with only places left upstairs. When I got upstairs I could hardly see if any of the seats were free due to the blanket of cigarette smoke. You could not see the front of the bus! The windows were running with condensation, and every other passenger, all old boys, were coughing their lungs up. Nice.

Usually, by some miracle the bus got to its destination, outside Pembroke Gate, in time for me to run to the ATC and clock on in time. But this was not going to be my preferred choice of travel.

The newly-acquired bike was better, but hard work. It was so much heavier than my other bike, and it felt as if going to work and coming home were both uphill. Because it was always raining, several layers of clothing made things more difficult. So it was time to save up and buy my first motorbike.

My sister had a girlfriend who had a small motorbike for sale, a Royal Enfield 125cc, so I purchased this 'bag of bolts' for £18. I'm sure that bike was female! It would go if it wanted to, but not otherwise. I cleaned, repainted, and serviced it, but basically it was an old, knackered two-stroke. I went to the Dockyard College on it one day and went home to Rainham in the lunch hour, when it broke down. This time it was the cylinder head gasket that had blown, so I made a new one from an old cocoa tin, and it worked! It was still on the bike when it went to the scrapyard.

That bike was always letting me down. I had my mate Dudley Young to thank for saving my bacon by giving me a lift in on many occasions. He lived at the top of our road and when I could not start the bloody Enfield I would rush out, flag him down and beg a lift on his trusty Lambretta.

The weeks passed, and just before the Easter break we had a visitor. A mouse had been seen several times in the workshop and several hilarious attempts were made to catch it. It probably came in because we ate sitting on our toolboxes in the workshop, and it had found some scraps. A concerted effort was made to catch the little blighter by blocking off all its known exit holes and collecting a range of weapons - hammers, heavy spanners, etc – for use as missiles as and when it appeared.

About a week after his first appearance the mouse was struck by a thrown hammer and killed instantly. One of the apprentices (presumably he had planned this) went into the unoccupied instructors' office and emerged with Eddie T's tobacco pouch. The mouse, bleeding profusely, was ceremoniously buried in the tobacco and the pouch buttoned up. When we left at the end of the day the pouch was left behind a corner radiator, just out of sight.

When we came back to work after Easter the place stank. The mouse had cooked in the tobacco in the pouch, and was now decomposing. The instructors were at first at a loss to work out where the foul smell was coming from, but it didn't take them too long - they just followed their noses. The tobacco pouch was ruined, and needless to say no one ever owned up to the misdemeanour.

By this time we were all regular visitors to the factory, not just to obtain consumable stores such as chalk and emery paper for our training needs. We had also come to realize that it was a permanent source of nuts, bolts etc. for repairing our bikes or motorbikes.

On one such visit we were talking to the stores assistant, who explained that the main office above his stores had originally been the Inspector's office (there was only one for the whole of the factory at this time). The Inspector's name was Mr Batty. He was a man of the old school, only just inferior to God. He was never seen without his bowler hat, and when he descended to the factory shop floor, everybody made sure they looked busy.

By this time several of the apprentices had acquired motorcycles. I for my part had to look for another, after disaster struck the Royal Enfield. One day when it refused to start I decided to try to bump-start it; I had discovered that the flywheel magneto was knackered. I ran alongside the thing, in gear, clutch disengaged, and jumped on. As I put my foot on the footrest the whole bottom half of the engine's frame collapsed and fell with a noisy CLANG into the middle of the road. The thing had been badly repaired by brazing and painted over, providing sufficient camouflage until some sucker (me) bought it. I sold it in bits to Frank Miers, a motorcycle parts dealer in New Road, Chatham, for scrap value.

So I now needed a new motor bike, and I found just the thing, a nice 350cc BSA model B31 at Grays of Chatham. I had to sell almost everything I owned to find the deposit - record player, bike, fishing rods etc - but I raised the deposit and signed the HP agreement.

One of the apprentices, Jim Apps, got himself a rather unusual 'Indian Brave' motor bike. When he first brought it to work we all crowded around, as was the custom, to inspect this machine, and Vic Salmon and I decided that we should road test it. Jim took some persuading, but he eventually agreed, so we took it out at lunchtime and did a performance test along the Power House straight. I was 'driving', with Vic as the passenger, as at that time you were allowed to ride pillion inside the dockyard. The road test was a complete failure, mainly because the bike had a very unusual hand gear change. Although we screamed the engine, we never got it out of first gear and only achieved 17 miles per hour. I don't think it did the motorbike's gearbox much good.

Jim was a smashing fella, but he was not hot on hygiene and used to chuck up a bit, especially in summer. He invariable wore a PVC Belstaff type motorcycle jacket, which we all blamed for causing his problem. It didn't seem to worry him too much – in fact he used to refer to himself as 'BO Apps'.

My mates had also got themselves motorbikes by this time. Vic

Salmon had a BSA B31 like mine, while Dave (Panda) was very lucky - his dad bought him a brand new Norton Model 50. Paddy had a 500cc Velocette Venom. We often went out as a group.

My first experiences with the BSA were not encouraging. It was delivered by Grays and left in the back garden waiting for me when I got home. Naturally both parents accompanied me out to see the new arrival. Grays had parked it for me on the centre stand on the path in the back garden. The path was raised above the garden on either side, so when I sat on the bike and pushed it forward off the stand, I could not reach the garden with my right leg. I lost my balance and the bike fell over, with me still on it. I then realized what a heavy old beast this machine was, and the importance of keeping your balance. I think it was at this time that my parents started to worry about my involvement with motorbikes.

It didn't get any better. That night was a Monday and we used to meet on Mondays at a youth club in the Central Hall at Chatham. Several guys from work knew that I would be turning up on my new bike, and were waiting outside for me to arrive, as was my current girlfriend Carol.

I wanted to make a real entrance. Although it was raining heavily, I decided to leave the braking late and stop by coming down through the gearbox. Plenty of noise - get everyone's attention - good plan. But I hadn't thought this through - first ride on the bike, wet road, no idea of the gear ratios. Guess what happened next? I changed up through the gears too quickly, the back wheel locked, the bike slid one way and me the other. My mates slid off inside the club to spare me even more embarrassment (or to have a quiet chuckle) and it was left to a couple of sailors standing outside an adjacent pub to pick me and the bike up off the road. Not an auspicious start!

The bike wasn't badly damaged (in contrast to my pride) - the footrest was bent and some superficial scratches, but otherwise it was OK. I sulked all evening and was glad when it was going home time.

I could only afford the HP for the motorbike because I still had my other job. From the age of 13, I had been working on Friday nights, Saturday all day and evenings as required at the Rainham Mark Stores, delivering groceries and greengroceries to the surrounding area. I used a tradesman's bike, which had a large carrier over the front wheel, during the week and on Saturdays and accompanied the van driver, Derek (my brother-in-law), doing the deliveries on Friday nights. It was a good job, and I met a lot of nice people including a couple of early girlfriends. The boss, Mr Settatree, was a real gentleman. While I was still at school this job had proved a real boon, as the Christmas tips given to me by the customers used to largely pay for exchange trips to Germany with my school.

The pay was 1s 3d per hour (the same as I was earning in the dockyard). This was great and I loved the job, but unfortunately the shop was soon to close, due to a new Co-Op opening up almost next door, so I just hoped that it would last until I got a pay rise at the dockyard.

One of the perks of the delivery job was that you got to see all the girls going out on Saturday, and this was how I met one of my first girlfriends, Joan. She was a lovely girl, and went on to marry one of my mates, Harry.

After several months in the dockyard we were getting to be old hands. One of the most unsettling things about the job was the routine police searches at going home time, to check we hadn't been nicking anything. Although you had nothing to hide you still felt guilty. What normally happened was that you were selected ('tapped', as it was known) and shepherded into the search station. Here another police officer would ask 'Do you have any Crown property on your person?' he would normally then 'tap you down' and search your lunch bag. Your car or motorbike would also be searched before you were allowed to proceed.

Mostly this was done quite pleasantly and quickly, but I knew it didn't pay to be a 'wise guy' with the police as they could keep you there for ages if you displayed an attitude.

On our exploratory walks around the yard we discovered all sorts of new and interesting things. As soon as you entered Pembroke Gate you saw the stables where the huge shire-type horses were stabled. These were used by a firm called Curtis, who used them to collect and carry large and heavy items within the yard, and for general housekeeping duties.

The main workshops in this area included the blacksmiths, patternmakers, painters, electrical, light plate, hose, shipwrights, no. 5 machine shop, bottle and fridge shops; the dockyard laboratory, garage and the central (no. 3) canteen. A strange mixture of other buildings housed the personnel department, the surgery, compressor and boiler houses, the laundry, no. 3 dockyard well, the bosun's blockhouse workshop, the yard services in the old power station building, and the Property Services Agency (PSA) workshops and offices. Clocking on/off sheds (muster stations) were located at strategic locations for the workforce. Police offices and search areas were located just inside the Pembroke Gate and replicated at the other entrance gates.

One of the problems when a group of young lads are together is that they will get up to mischief, and on one occasion this nearly proved disastrous. Near the training centre was a storage area for very large electrical cable drums. Some of these were 10 feet in diameter and fully enclosed on the outer rim except for a gap of about 18' where the cable had been removed. These were ideal 'toys' for some of the bigger and older apprentices in their lunch hours. One of them had the bright idea of forcing an unsuspecting 'appo' (apprentice) into one of these cable drums through the small opening, and before he could struggle out, rolling the drum away with the poor appo inside yelling and hollering. This was great fun, for when the victim was eventually released he was so dizzy that he could not stand up straight or walk in a straight line, and was sometimes sick. I believe this little prank was called 'preparing for spaceflight'.

What fun it was - until the day when it all went horribly wrong. On this particular day the usual thing happened, a lad was put inside the cable drum and several others pushed it as hard as they could. What was different on this day was that the drum was being rolled along the road beside the sea wall, and as it reached maximum speed it hit a house brick in the road and the whole drum veered off at a sharp angle towards the sea wall. Utter panic.

The drum, with the lad still inside, hit the three-foot high sea wall and rose up on to it, balancing on top and inching towards the 30-foot drop into the water on the other side. Luckily a guard chain is situated along the seawall at this point, and it was this which I am convinced saved the boy's life.

The cable drum rocked momentarily in the 12 o'clock position, then very very slowly rolled backwards into the road. The dozen or so of us watching, holding our breath, hearts pounding, could all have done with a change of underpants.

Unfortunately the problems were not over. The lad inside the drum was aware that there had been a problem, although not the magnitude of it, and decided that it was a good time to get out. Unfortunately the drum had not stopped rolling, and as he poked his head out to exit, the drum continued to roll, squashing his head between the drum and the ground. The drum did one more rotation before it was brought to a complete standstill, and the shocked, battered, and very bruised apprentice fell out. His head had been badly squeezed, and the skin on his face had been pulled and stretched very badly, but he had not sustained any serious injuries. He was unbelievably lucky; he could have died twice.

He was taken to the surgery for checks as a precautionary measure, but was passed as OK after treatment for abrasions, cuts and shock. That particular game was not played again.

There were lighter moments. Sadly at this time the actress

Kay Kendall died, and this was covered in the newspapers, along with a very attractive picture of her. One of the lads, Micky Pierce, was seen going into the toilet with the newspaper, and several of the other apprentices crept up outside the toilet door to listen. The story was that there was much rustling of the newspaper accompanied by other 'suspicious' noises, so word went out that he was having a wank! He was of course, subjected to almost unbearable piss-taking concerning this for weeks after, and his denials only acted to confirm our suspicions.

I remember another incident well. Joe Ward was on the receiving end of one of Dick Seamark's pranks when he was repairing one of the workshop vices. He had supported the vice handle with a large block of wood and was using a large hammer to rivet over the nut on the opposite end, while the handle was being steadied by his free hand. Joe was taking heavy swipes at this, completely unaware that Dick had crawled underneath the bench from the other side and was waiting for him to take the next swing.

As Joe took a mighty swing at the repair he was attempting, Dick kicked away the block of wood which was supporting the vice handle. As Joe hit the top of the handle, now unsupported, it slid downwards at a rapid rate and pinched Joe's hand between the two components. The injured hand started to swell up immediately, and a very large, ugly blood blister formed at the place of impact. Joe hopped around like an agitated dervish, shaking the injured arm and shouting 'Fuck a pig lad, Fuck a pig!' This was one of his favourite expressions in times of stress.

We had difficulty making our wages last, so as the weekend approached money was usually very short. Sometimes if we had enough on a Thursday we would treat ourselves to a night at the 'Bughutch' (the Royal Cinema in Rainham), which would cost us 2s 3 ½d (two and threepence halfpenny) - two shillings to get in and three and a half pence for fruit gums. We knew how to live! Sometimes we could talk my brother-in-law into coming for a pint with us (me and Paddy Hargan at this time) at the Belisha Beacon pub, for a game of darts, but he would have to lend us ten bob each until payday. Usually Thursday evenings were spent cleaning our motorbikes at my home (Paddy was in 'digs'), meticulously cleaning every component and then polishing the chrome and aluminium with Solvol Autosol. After a couple of hours or so we would go into Mum's kitchen, up to our elbows in oil and grease, use up half her tin of Vim and leave the sink dirty.

Paddy shared his digs with Taffy Roberts, another apprentice. In the early days we would often cycle home together. One such day I had just got past Gillingham station when I caught up with Paddy, off his bike at the end of an alley and looking agitated. 'What's up?' I asked, to be told that Taff had been in an argument with someone and they had gone into the alley to sort it out.

We went into the alley to investigate, and found Taff and the other guy, who was perhaps in his forties and of medium build, squaring up to each other. 'Box him Taff!' we urged. But BANG BANG, the other bloke had hit Taff twice before he could move. 'Wrestle him Taff!' we suggested, but again the old guy had Taff squirming in pain in an arm lock, no trouble at all.

It was handbags really, and Taff wasn't badly hurt (except his pride), but I think we all learned not to mouth off to people unless we were sure of the outcome. The guy explained that he had had boxing and wrestling experience when he was in the Navy.

Towards the end of the first year I had a nasty motorbike accident and was very lucky to escape without serious injuries, or worse. Three of us were riding out to Chatham in our lunch break in convoy, racing to be the first into town. We were all travelling up Dock Road, overtaking slower vehicles, me in front. I remember overtaking a bus, and the next thing I knew I was lying on the pavement on the opposite side of the road face down. Apparently a motorcycle and sidecar had been in front of the bus, and just as I got alongside he pulled out. Our handlebars clashed and I was sent into the air, bounced once and ricocheted onto the path. My motorbike carried on up the road until it finally crashed into the dockyard wall.

I was able to sit up after a short while and check if anything was hanging off. I was obviously very badly shaken and had suffered severe abrasions to my face (no crash helmet, as these were not yet compulsory), knees, ankles, elbows and back. But nothing was broken and there was no serious injury. Lucky boy! I had missed hitting a car travelling in the opposite direction by seconds - I would probably have gone through his windscreen.

My mates had stopped and helped me prop myself against the wall. Someone produced a cloth to cover my facial abrasions, and someone else dragged my motorbike into a safe area. An ambulance had already been called. I remember sitting on the roadside, holding the pad to my face and feeling pretty lousy, when I happened to notice one of the senior apprentices, who I knew vaguely, ride past looking at me with a huge smirk on his face. Nice fella!

The ambulance arrived quite quickly and I remember getting Vic Salmon, one of my mates on this trip, to promise to convince my parents that I was going to be OK. He was going to see them with the 'good news' before he returned to work.

One of the other apprentices, Jim Apps, had only just arrived as I was being taken away in the ambulance. He looked at my motorbike and jumped to the wrong conclusion. He went back to work and told them all I had been killed!

The first year's training was now coming to an end, with all of us having reached the required standard. We now had a feel for the role of the dockyard and our place in it. I for my part had not experienced any problems in acquiring the necessary craft and academic skills, but I was still having difficulty getting to work on time, often being late by a minute or two. I was also struggling to make our two weeks' holiday last for the whole year. These problems were to stay with me for some time yet.

CHAPTER 2

YEAR TWO: THE 'BOTTLE SHOP'

We did our second year of training in the 'Bottle Shop'. Actually it was a small corner of the workshop which had been cordoned off as an apprentices' training area. To the side through the wire-mesh partition we could often see the large high-pressure air bottles being 'rumbled'. This process is basically to fill the bottles, which were usually 9.1 cu ft. (very large) high pressure air vessels, with small pieces of sharp steel plate and rotate them on a very large turntable. The steel plates inside the bottle then would scour and clean the bottle internally.

Our dedicated area comprised much of the same equipment as we had had in the previous workshop, with benches with drawers and vices along each side and at the top of our work area.

There were also several training aids: engines, various types of valves, pumps, compressors and other major assemblies, which had sections cut away to show exploded views of the internal components. On the walls were a copy of the Factories Act and some very old, tired looking safety posters.

Immediately outside the main entrance were a large cycle rack and a toilet block. This was when I first became aware of the jealously-guarded pecking order of the toilets. The main toilet block was marked 'Workmen', but to the rear two more, smaller toilets were identified as 'Chargeman's Toilet' and 'Inspector's Toilet'.

This really annoyed me. Why was it necessary for the 'officers' to have their own dedicated toilets? Did my shit stink more than theirs? I often asked this question, but never got a satisfactory answer. Guess which toilets I used when the need arose? Perhaps I had delusions of grandeur.

My timekeeping had not improved much, and I was still very prone to being a minute or so late. This was going to be a problem, as the Time Recorder (who checks that the clock is accurate and oversees the workmen clocking in) at this workshop was a real bastard. His name was Hewson. He took a particular dislike to me, probably because of my cavalier approach and my constant enquiries concerning his parenthood. On several occasions I was dashing towards the clock to beat the 7.30 deadline (new start time), only to see him nudge the minute hand on so that I clocked on late. Again. Some of the recorders were quite sympathetic towards marginally latecomers (not only me) and would hold the clock for one or two minutes to save people being late (and losing pay), but not this one.

On one such day when I was racing to beat the clock, one of the other apprentices, Alan West, had just clocked on and was standing by the workshop entrance. When he saw me arriving in a hurry on my motorbike he grabbed the bike and said 'I've got your bike - go and clock on, you'll just make it'. I didn't - 7.31 again!

Worse was to follow. When I got outside, I saw that Alan had been unable to hold my motorbike upright and it had fallen against the cycle-rack. Disaster.

The lovely paintwork and chrome on the petrol tank had been damaged, and although most of it polished out with no dents, I was a very unhappy Teddy. Alan was also distraught; it wasn't really his fault. He had a much smaller bike, and was just not used to the extra weight - my bike weighed 420lbs.

Our two instructors for this period of our training were Tom Russell and Mr Searle. Mr Searle (I can't remember his first name, if I ever knew it) was in the standard instructors mould: average height, stocky and probably in his middle fifties. He was ex-Navy, smoked a lot, and was not of a very cheerful disposition, but this may have been because, as we had been told, he had health problems. A stomach injury sustained in wartime?

Tom Russell was something else. He believed he was the bee's knees, and had done everything and been everywhere. Some of his stories were unbelievable, and after a while we stopped listening - compared to Tom, Eddie Turner was on a truth drug! However what he did have was good technical knowledge and good instructional technique. He also had quite a cheerful personality. Again our craft training was supplemented by occasional lectures, these being held in the workshop.

One day we were given a lecture on magnetos (the

component used to produce the spark for petrol engines), when one of the group discovered that if you wound the handle on the training aid and held on to its HT lead you got quite a sharp electric shock. So of course after that all of us, a group of six or more, had to hold hands while someone wound the handle as fast as they could so that we all got an electric shock. They say little things please little minds!

By this time we were starting to feel a little happier about our chosen careers. We had completed our first year of training, and the second year was less regimented, giving us, we felt, an element of freedom. Also we had the comedians to keep us happy. One of the comics was Pete Appleby. He was a naturally funny guy anyway, with a permanent smile on his face, and a nose that had been broken and now permanently looked left. His dry humour and original witticisms had us permanently amused. It wasn't just what he said that was funny, but the way that he did things.

I remember one cold winter morning Pete arrived for work a little late, seeming a bit agitated. As he took off his heavy motorcycle jacket to put on his overalls we could all see that the seat of his trousers had been ripped out, showing a shredded pair of underpants and a large expanse of muddy bum. He also had bad grazes on his bum cheeks, clearly visible through the damaged clothing, but it was such a funny sight that he got no sympathy at all. He had fallen off his motorbike on his way to work and skidded along the road on his backside. With only minor injuries to his bottom and his pride he was soon back to his old self, although he did say that it was bloody cold going home that night.

We now got occasional visits from some of the apprentices in the other intakes (entries), and when the opportunity arose they would call to catch up on all the latest happenings. This was when I first encountered Paul Kenyon ('Mad Yon'), a character who was MUCH larger than life. I still don't believe some of the things he did, although I was there!

Paul used to be very popular with the other apprentices, as he had supreme self confidence and a strong personality, and he would try anything. He also had an ever-changing supply of pornographic postcards, which were very much appreciated by us art experts. He had made friends with Tommy Nye, the 'dirty book' man in the factory, who loaned his books to Paul so that our education was improved even further; just the thing for rampant 17-year-olds!

One Monday morning Paul came to work raving about a girl he had met at the weekend. Lucy was a goddess, and Paul was in love. Unfortunately she had gone on holiday to Cornwall for a week. Paul could not stand the thought of a whole week without her, but he had no transport.

One of the senior group of lads who visited us on a regular basis was Cyril Moffat, and Cyril had a new moped. He had bought it about three weeks earlier as a cheap form of transport to work; a brand new shiny 'Norman Nippy'.

Now you might not think a 50cc moped is a suitable form of transport to go to Cornwall on, but this didn't seem to worry Paul at all. The only problem that Paul had now was to persuade Cyril to lend him his (almost) brand new moped. It took nearly all week, but his constant pleas and cast-iron promises to respect the moped finally did the trick (no doubt some money changed hands as well), and Paul set off early on Friday morning to travel to the caravan park where his girlfriend was holidaying in Cornwall.

When Paul came in to work on the Monday morning he looked terrible. His eyes were badly bloodshot and so badly puffed up that they looked half closed. He was also in a foul mood. It took a couple of days to drag the story out of him. Roughly, this is what had happened.

He had left early on Friday morning, and the journey had been a complete nightmare. The ride down to Cornwall took 14 hours. This meant that apart from stopping twice at public toilets (we still had them then) for a quick wee, he remained all that time in a sitting position, arms stretched out in front, while the little machine beneath him was being thrashed mercilessly, the vibrations running back up his arms to his armpits. It had been like driving a pneumatic drill for two days. And he had no goggles, only sunglasses.

When at last he found the caravan site, it was completely dark. He was cold beyond description and could hardly stand after so long in the same riding position. He was also starving hungry and exhausted. He fell off the moped outside the girl's caravan, staggered up to the door and knocked. No answer - they were out! He almost cried with disappointment and fatigue.

Nearby was a large toilet block which he had noticed on the

way in. He staggered over to it and found refuge in one of the cubicles. It was warm and dry, but unfortunately it meant he had to resume the sitting position he had been forced into all day long.

Paul slept, sort of, for a couple of hours, then decided to see if Lucy was back yet. He went back to the caravan and saw that a light was on. It was now 10.30. He knocked again - no answer. He knocked again, louder this time. After a couple of minutes the door was opened by a large man, with a not-too-amused expression on his face.

'What do you want?' he asked, in a less than friendly, almost aggressive manner.

'I'm Paul, Lucy's boyfriend, and I've come to see her' Paul explained pleadingly.

'Well you can just bugger off. I don't want you young boys hanging around my daughter, and if I see you again you'll be sorry. Now get lost!'

Paul was so exhausted and so disillusioned with the whole episode that he did not have the will to argue. He felt like crying. Not exactly the welcome he had been expecting. He was stuck in a caravan park, in Cornwall, late on a Friday night, knackered, cold, hungry and depressed. There was nothing else he could do but head back to the toilet cubicle again and get his head down.

He got a few hours' sleep from sheer exhaustion, and awoke with every muscle in his body screaming for mercy. He didn't bother to try to see Lucy again. Then it was back on the moped, throttle full open, to suffer the torturous miles back home. He recovered quite quickly from the ordeal, but various versions of this trip kept us lads amused for several weeks.

Now that we had motorbikes we had a choice of what to do in the dinner hour. If we had the inclination, and any money, we could go for a little ride. Alternatively, if the weather was OK, a walk around the dockyard would prove very interesting. The first time you see a ship being 'docked down' can be quite a sight. The ship is manoeuvred into dock, the caisson (the 'gate' which fits into the dock entrance) is placed into position and the water is pumped out. This must be done with the ship held in the correct location, supported at both sides and critically beneath the keel. It is quite a complicated procedure, and relies on a high level of co-ordination and teamwork. Likewise when large vessels entered through the lock gates (the main entrance from the river Medway into the Dockyard) into the main basins, it was an interesting spectacle, and you had to admire the skills required.

The full variety of workshops and activities were now opened up to us. There was a ropery, which still made all the Navy's rope (sisal and nylon) requirements, and did repayment work – making rope to be sold to industry.

The Sail and Colour loft made flags and bunting for many foreign governments as well as for the Navy. The laundry cleaned the coveralls for the workforce. The smithery, galvanising shop, covered slips, machine shops, the workshops for coppersmiths, plumbers, fitters, electricians, boilermakers, sailmakers, shipwrights, caulkers and riveters, patternmakers, joiners, painters, laggers, weapons, slingers - and no doubt some I've missed! There were vast storehouses, office blocks, yard services, MT garage, canteens and much more.

The other option at lunchtime, usually the preferred one, was to nip out on your bike. This brought pleasures twofold. First you could get away from your place of work for an hour's break, and secondly there was the sheer thrill of getting on the motorbike and blasting away in the fresh air, with no noise and fumes and no boring repetitive work.

Quite often we would visit the home of one my mates, Bob Webb. Bob and I had been to the Technical School together and had been mates since. We would call at his mum's, usually two or three of us, and she would lash us up with egg and chips – heaven. She was a really lovely lady, and far from complaining she really seemed to enjoy us visiting, albeit always at mealtimes!

Now that we were wealthy second-year apprentices we could afford to push the boat out, and we would sometimes seek out a favourite café for a quick cup of tea and do a bit of posing. One of these lunchtimes will stay in my memory forever. Our favourite haunt at that time was the Rainbow Café, near Luton Arches (Chatham). We would go there for reasons of bravado, as we were told that this was a place some of the local 'tabbies' (working girls) frequented.

We duly arrived, parked up, and sure enough one of the local girls, who with her sister was quite well known, was there sitting on a bar stool up at the counter. She didn't pay much attention to us as we went in other than perhaps to give a rather amused smile. We sat there for some time sipping our tea, smoking our tailor-made ciggies (well, it was a Friday) and trying to pretend we weren't trying to look up her very short skirt (this was before ultra-short skirts were fashionable). After we had been there for about 10 minutes, by which time we were getting rather hot under the collar, Jackie (that was the girl's name), got off the bar stool, presumably to leave. However, as she swung herself off the stool she pulled her handbag off the counter and it snagged on the back of the next stool. Her handbag opened and a flat tin spun through the air and landed in the middle of the floor with a clatter. The lid opened and three condoms rolled out in different directions. Jackie laughed, bent over and picked up the 'johnnies' to put them back into the tin, also reclaiming a brush and other items which had been thrown out of her bag. Two of us sat there with mouths open while the other went scarlet (he was good at this).

We were never quite sure if this incident was in fact an accident, or perhaps a very ingenious marketing ploy. If so it was wasted on us, as we could not have afforded her even if we had pooled our money. In fact we would have run like hell if 'it' had been offered.

Another café we used was in Canterbury Street, Gillingham, where I had an embarrassing experience one Friday lunchtime. I had bought a rather nice leather motorcycle jacket from one of the other apprentices, and customized it with a design in bifurcated rivets. Pleased with this, my next adornment to the jacket was a nice brass star, a copy of the BSA motif, which I had made at work and had engraved just like the real thing.

Now to the embarrassing bit. Having got myself seated in the café, rather proud of the bright shiny new star adorning the jacket, I was devastated to hear the biggest guy in the café, who looked like trouble, call out: 'Sheriff, hey Sheriff!' He was obviously enjoying the joke with his mates, and my embarrassment. Ignoring him didn't help. He persisted, so we didn't stop long on that day and the badge came off.

My timekeeping unfortunately had not improved. I was still late occasionally and this had resulted in warnings. Mostly this was for being just one or two minutes late, but in the eyes of my employer I was Late On Parade, and this was unacceptable. Eventually I was put on 'Prompt Muster'. This meant that no lateness at all was acceptable and that if I did not clock on before the allotted time, I would not be permitted to start work and would be sent home. This shock treatment worked to a certain extent, but I did slip up occasionally and lost a morning's pay. It was taking me a long time to see the bigger picture and to understand the rules of the game.

We did about eight months' training in the bottle shop, and then we were sent into the factory to start training on machine tools – lathes, milling machines, etc. It all started with training on centre lathes in a dedicated apprentices' training area in the centre of the factory. This was where we learned the basics of turning, facing and thread-cutting materials, and how to read, measure and manufacture items from engineering drawings. Again the training became very boring, because of the repetitive nature of the tasks, and one day it nearly ended in disaster.

We were preparing for our first machining test job, a repetitive activity which involved cutting a special multi-start thread. The workpiece was being driven by a mandrel, which as it rotated protruded above the headstock of the lathe. This job got very boring, and Dick Seamark, training on the lathe in front of me, had become almost mesmerized by the slow rotation of the machine.

He rested his forearm along the top of the lathe and was about to make himself comfortable, head on forearm, when the mandrel, spinning on the lathe, caught the sleeve of his overall and violently pulled his arm to the back of the machine. Fortunately his overalls had torn, otherwise the lathe would have tried to wind his arm around the workpiece.

He shouted out in alarm, and luckily his arm was released as the overalls tore. We had all been taught how to switch off the machines in an emergency, which one of the apprentices had done, but it would have been much too late if the overalls had not torn; Dick would have been badly injured, and possibly lost his arm. He was taken to the surgery for a check-up and treated for shock. The rest of us could well have been treated for shock as well. It certainly put a damper on proceedings for the rest of the day, and we were all extremely careful running our lathes for several days afterwards. Dick was only away from work for about a week, but he did come in to see us after a couple of days, arm in a sling, and his beaming smile returned.

Proudly, although somewhat gingerly, he showed us the injured arm beneath the sling. The whole of the arm on the inside from armpit to wrist was a massive black bruise - ruptured blood vessels, we were told. We couldn't believe how lucky he was.

At about the same time as we started the lathe test job, the adjacent section, which was an engine testing area, began a series of test runs. This meant that the massive engines which were fitted into submarines were being run up less than 50 yards away. Can you imagine the noise they made? It was common knowledge that these engines could be heard running, if the wind was in a favourable direction, as far away as Bluebell Hill five miles away. It should also be explained that we were not issued with ear defenders, as health and safety was very basic at that time.

The other major problem created by these engines was the vibration they caused. We were trying to do precision machining work and take exact measurements with a massive engine thumping away alongside of us! I remember complaining to my family, after riding home from work on my bike, that I could still hear the noise of these engines thumping away in my ears for at least an hour after I got home.

CHAPTER 3

YEAR THREE: IN PRODUCTION

Having successfully completed our test jobs at the end of our training on the lathes, we were all sent out to work, for the first time as individuals, under the supervision of 'skippers' in the production sections of the factory, to further improve on our basic skills.

I was sent to the milling section. My skipper, Laurie, was a small man, originally from Egypt, who spoke fairly good English but was generally very quiet and only spoke to answer. But he was a good skipper, and explained very well how to operate the machine and what to do.

It should probably be explained at this point that the majority of craftsmen were not keen to take on apprentices. There were several reasons for this. The dockyard pay scheme included provision to earn extra money by way of a bonus scheme (known colloquially as 'ticket'); the faster you completed the job to the required standard, the more money you earned. Obviously when you were training an apprentice it slowed you down, even if he was interested and able, so although you as craftsman would receive a training allowance, which I think at this time it was about £1 per week, you might in fact lose money because of the longer time it took to do your job.

The other drawback with training an apprentice of course was that they would often get bored very quickly, and if their mates came to visit they usually got into mischief. So the skipper had to be aware of what 'the lad' was up to, all of the time.

The consequence of this was that some of the skippers had very little interest in training the lads. In fact it was often the less competent fitters who took on an apprentice, purely to get the extra £1 a week. This of course is the same in every walk of life, in terms of fitters and apprentices; there are the good, the not-so-good and the indifferent.

I can only remember one job I had on the milling machines, which was to machine the hexagonal heads on some special bolts. I probably remember this as it was the first job I worked on in the bonus scheme (ticket). Laurie had given me this job to do on my own and I loved it. I worked like stink on that job, getting it finished in very good time, and about three weeks later the bonus pay, about £5, came through: an extra week's money. I was over the moon.

Funny also how you remember details. Laurie used to eat garlic by the shedload every lunchtime, and you had to keep clear in the afternoon because his breath was 'radioactive'.

The training period on this section soon passed and it was time to move on again. My next training period would be at the other end of the factory on section 34, Valves and Auxiliaries. Two of us apprentices were sent to this section, me and Paddy Hargan. We were allocated to skippers; mine was Dick Marsh and Paddy was to work with Jack Hayter. This worked very well because Dick and Jack were great mates and so were Paddy and I. We had plenty of interesting work to keep us occupied, so the days were busy but enjoyable.

Jack was about 60 at this time, average height, quite slim, short grey hair (although mostly bald), and very thick 'Mr Magoo' type glasses. He had a wicked sense of humour and a seemingly endless repertoire of profound and usually comical expressions. One of his favourites, if he caught us on a break was 'Procrastination is the thief of time'.

The other nugget that he often offered Paddy was 'if you're going courting in the countryside boy, always make sure you know where to find a five-bar gate'. The first time he offered this advice, Paddy and I decided that we needed more information. 'Well' said Jack, 'in the country a five-bar gate is what is known as an adjustable fanny. If you are out with a short girl you sit her on the top bar when you do it, and the tall girls go on the bottom' He would then chuckle to himself as if he was reminiscing, shoulders bouncing up and down as he enjoyed the moment.

Dick was shorter and quite tubby. Usually a cheerful sort, you could see him as a favourite uncle. He was more of a listener than a talker, and you could often see his shoulders moving gently as he giggled quietly at one of Jack's pearls of wisdom. He was a pipe smoker and when he used to flash up this fearsome beast, usually at break times, he would completely disappear in a blanket of foul-smelling smoke, like some magician's stage act. A very kind man, he was also very proud of his trade skills and pleased to pass on his expertise to his apprentice 'wards'.

Both Jack and Dick used to pull our legs concerning our attempted successes with the opposite sex, requesting blow-by-blow reports the following morning. Both of us had casual, non-regular girlfriends at this time, so there was very little to report, but we both had vivid imaginations. I'm sure they realized that most of our reports owed more than a little to poetic licence.

When the valves we had refitted were finished they would be sent to an adjacent section to be tested. The item to be tested was bolted down on to a water pressure test rig and subjected to the required pressure (at least the same as that it would be working at); this was very interesting, as you could see immediately the results of your recent efforts.

After approximately four months we had refitted most types of valves that were fitted in the warships, and it was time to move to the next training section. The next section I was sent to was Auxiliary Equipments, or as I soon rechristened it, 'Land of the Dead'. Unfortunately this section had been run down to such an extent that it was now just a parking spot for the unfortunates. My skipper, one of the few on the section who was still alive, was a small North Country guy named Lou Rainer. He did his best to look after me, but the truth of the matter was that we had no work to do. If you have ever been in a situation where you have no work but have to pretend to be busy when a supervisor is about, you will understand that it is (a) hard work, and (b) soul destroying.

Others on the section were really scary. The guy who 'worked' nearest to me, on the next bench, was called Matthew Hannah, and he was obviously unwell. He was always at work by the time I got there (nothing unusual in that, so was everybody else) but he would be sitting next to a radiator resting his head on his fearnought (a seaman's jacket similar to a duffle coat) and seemed to be half asleep. He would stay like that for the rest of the day. When I asked Lou what was wrong with Matthew he would just say that he had some big problems, and was not well. To be honest Matthew used to scare me rigid, his eyes always looked haunted.

He certainly was not well. Unfortunately, while I was on this section, Matthew committed suicide. Apparently he went home one night and gassed himself. As was the custom then, his tools were sold off at work with the proceeds going to the widow or family. I still have some of his tools today, engraved with his initials. What made this situation even worse was that a few years later his son did exactly the same thing!

One of the other fitters on this section was even stranger. He was nicknamed 'blueskin' (I know not why and I certainly did not ask). The story was that he had at one time been the top diesel engine fitter in the dockyard. Some time before I had joined this section his wife had died and this had triggered off his strange behaviour. He was a large man, of scruffy appearance with a full head of grey hair, and I would estimate that he was in his late sixties.

It was his going-home ritual that we found odd. About half

an hour before clocking-off time he would get his cup from a shelf in the centre of the section, and with a token attempt to shelter himself he would get his cock out and piss into it. He would take a good look at the results, then remove his dentures and give them a good flush in the urine. Satisfied that they were now properly cleaned, he would pop them back into his mouth. He would then disappear to change out of his overalls, prior to the outmuster. When he returned to the section he would be wearing a pair of women's shoes, not high heels but with a heel, and as he tottered about, not too elegantly, we could see that he had put stockings on as well. He then would complete his home-going preparations by putting on his lipstick!

It would not be unfair to say that the silly bugger was an ugly old so-and-so anyway, with a deeply craggy face, and when this lipstick was applied so very badly, a lot of it around his nose, he looked like Norman Bates' mother in *Psycho*.

This experience was quite frightening at first to a fairly green lad, but after the initial shock it left me with a feeling of great sadness that this once great old boy had become such a lost and tortured soul.

This was not a happy section; I learned little and afterwards referred to it as the 'home of the bewildered'. One consolation was that as we had little work to do, a blind eye was turned when we went missing for fifteen minutes or so to visit our mates on the other sections. There was also the possibility that this gave us a chance to find out what the other sections' work entailed, and where the various operations were carried out. One of the most popular visits was to see Tommy Nye (the dirty book man) on the Turret lathes section. His vast collection of porno magazines, postcards and books were an exciting revelation to us young apprentices. Usually somewhere on the scene Paul Kenyon would be found bartering or exchanging the latest masterpieces with Tom. Both connoisseurs, they would gladly explain the finer points!

It was at this time that we apprentices learned the details of Paul's recent absence from work from a friend of his, 'Spud' Hudson. Paul had been absent for two weeks, and no one, even the instructors, seemed to know why. Gradually the story came out, although Spud had been sworn to secrecy.

Paul had had (another) row with his parents on the Friday night before his absence, and decided to leave home. As usual it was about the lack of money available to him, and therefore his inability to lead the lifestyle that he thought he was entitled to. Paul's parents were comparatively wealthy. Dad was an executive with BT and Mum had at least a couple of hairdressing shops, but they had decided that Paul should make his own way in life, so that he would appreciate the value of money.

It suited both parties that Paul should help out, on a paid basis, by collecting the week's takings from his mother's hairdressing shops on a Friday night. This particular Friday night apparently he had said 'sod it' and headed off to London in Mum's smart Jaguar with the week's takings from the two shops. On the Saturday afternoon Spud, Paul's mate, had a visit from him, with an invitation to spend the night on the town in

London, mostly all paid. They went to Paul's local pub, then on to a nightclub.

When they entered the nightclub, two of the hostesses hurried over to greet Paul with a 'Hi Paul' and kisses. These girls impressed Spud; they were gorgeous, smartly dressed and immaculately made up. It all seemed very sophisticated. They joined the boys for the rest of the evening, and of course they both drank champagne. Paul didn't seem to mind, as he obviously did not have a care in the world. It was early morning when three of them made their way by taxi, back to Paul's very nice hotel. Paul's companion was to spend the night with him. The other girl had made her excuses, much to Spud's relief, shortly before they had left the nightclub.

Spud had had a great time, which of course was the object of the exercise, and when Paul took him back home on Sunday morning he could not help felling somewhat jealous of the lifestyle Paul had to look forward to. But he was sworn not to reveal Paul's whereabouts to his parents, or to anyone else for that matter.

How quickly things can change. When Spud got the next visit from Paul on the following Saturday morning, something was obviously very wrong. Paul was not as bouncy as usual, and looking slightly dishevelled. At the earliest opportunity Paul pulled him to one side and asked 'Got anything to eat handy?' Spud's mum rustled up beans on toast in short time, and Paul quickly put it away.

The significance did not sink in at this point. Spud again

accompanied Paul up to London, but it was very different this time. He was now living in a squalid bedsit, sparsely furnished and freezing cold. On entering, Paul's opener was 'Have you got two bob for the meter, Spud?'

It was obvious that the money had all gone, with not even enough for little luxuries like food and heating. What a transformation, in just a week.

They had a walk around the local area, which wasn't very pleasant, and Paul borrowed ten shillings from Spud, which he invested in bread rolls and fillings. Paul gradually explained that he had had very little food all that week. It was, he said, only because he had befriended a couple of schoolgirls that he had managed to survive the week.

Paul had been leaving the digs early on Thursday morning when the two girls had walked past and given him the eye. Never one to miss an opportunity, he turned on his best chat-up lines. The girls were both probably both aged about fifteen, well developed, and looked to be carrying lunchbags. Neither of them seemed to be in a hurry to get to school.

Paul had explained that due to temporary, unfortunate circumstances he had run out of food and money, and asked them for food. 'What's in it for us?' the cheeky one had asked. Paul had said, not really joking 'You can have my body'. After much giggling the cheeky one said that suited her just fine, providing that her mate could watch.

Paul took them into his digs, and gave Cheeky a really good tubbing, which she made it very clear that she enjoyed, being very vocal with continuous encouragement like 'Come on Paul, give it to me hard, make me come, please make me come', as if he needed any encouragement. He had been turned on as soon as he saw that she was wearing navy blue knickers, something which he adored. All through the action, Cheeky's mate was getting more and more agitated, and at the end of the proceedings she disappeared into the next room for about five minutes, presumably to frig herself stupid. She looked happier when she came back.

Paul had himself a decent meal for a change, and both sets of sandwiches were very nice, or perhaps it was just that he was so hungry. The next day it was role reversal. The girls arrived early. Cheeky did the watching, offering lots of encouragement and advice, while her mate was even better. Perhaps this was due to a full day's anticipation, knowing that she was soon due a really powerful sex session, or perhaps she was like that anyway; they say you have to watch the quiet ones.

Paul certainly got more than he bargained for. It was the best and most uninhibited sex he had ever had, and I doubt if even he could have maintained this standard of performance for very long.

That did not matter, because the need would not arise. Paul had already decided that he would eat humble pie, go home and ask his parents to forgive and forget. There was another reason why he wanted to leave his digs. Paul had not used condoms in his sessions with the schoolgirls, and had given them the full flood of love-juice every time. He was conscious that this might well have serious repercussions in a few months' time, and did not want to be around to discuss the merits of unprotected sex with underage schoolgirls, with their parents and/or the police.

So it was home again to face the parents' wrath, but even this couldn't be straightforward for Paul. He got into Mum's Jag and set off for home, near Sittingbourne. All was fairly routine until he got to Blackheath. Travelling along the A2 he was overtaken by an American sports car, and as it passed alongside the driver looked at Paul, smiled and waved.

This was like a red rag to a bull. The two cars raced each other all the way along the A2 and through the Medway Towns at high speeds, overtaking in dangerous situations. Paul beat the sports car away from the traffic lights at the Luton Arches and gunned the Jag up Chatham Hill, doing about 70 miles an hour. Overtaking on the white line, he got halfway up the hill to where the road narrows when he met a small car, an Austin A35, travelling down the hill. The cars clipped each other and the A35 spun around and ended up facing in the opposite direction. Disaster.

By coincidence, and the worst possible luck, a young off-duty police officer was at the bus stop where the impact occurred. He must have thought that was his moment, and pounced. Unfortunately Paul was not the typical driver who had transgressed, and he answered the officer's requests for details by saying 'Don't let's make a federal case out of it John'. This did not go down too well in court, and Paul was banned for three years.

Paul returned home and ultimately was forgiven for his little escapade. He returned to work the following Monday and made his peace with the personnel office. It took us several weeks to wheedle out most of these sordid details piece by piece.

YEAR FOUR: WORKING AFLOAT

The last part of our apprenticeship would end the third year of our training. When we started the fourth year, my friend Bernard Hargan (Paddy) did not come to work afloat with us but was transferred to the MPBW (Ministry of Public Buildings and Works) instead. I am not sure if this was a matter of choice, luck of the draw, or because he was Irish. It must be remembered that the 'troubles' were ongoing at this time. He was transferred to the workshop just inside Pembroke Gate.

Paddy worked in the fitters' area, where he soon made good friends with Freddie Turner from the adjacent blacksmiths' section. The lads in this workshop were always looking to play jokes on unsuspecting passers-by, and I remember two of these from first-hand experience.

One prank was to superglue pins (standard paper pins), point upwards and at an angle, to the pavement outside the workshop. The lads would then loiter outside the shop until some poor unsuspecting fool (me on one occasion), stepped on to one of the pins. Your own weight would often drive the pin right through your shoe and into the foot. It didn't cause any major injury, just a very nasty shock, and it was hilarious to watch, no doubt.

The other little trick they often played was to get a small cardboard box, ideally say 4-6 inches square, fill it with lead pellets and leave it in the centre of the path outside of the workshop. As the road outside led to the main offices it would not be long before some young lad who fancied himself as a footballer would give the little box a hearty kick. The box would hardly move, but it sure gave the foot a nasty jolt!

I like to think these pranks were not meant to injure anyone, and they didn't, as far as I know. Although there were lots of girls and women who used this road, they were not stupid enough to go around kicking little boxes! We apprentices found this workshop was very useful if we needed a 'private' welding job done, or motorcycle footrests straightened in their forge.

To start my fourth year of training I was allocated to the Fitters Afloat 3 (FA3) and sent to work at 46 shop. This was a largish workshop located at the head of No. 4 Dock, in the south area of the dockyard. The workshop was split into two halves. The front half was the workshop proper, with large double doors for equipment access, and inside against the perimeter walls were attached large workbenches with heavy duty vices. The rear of the building was the 'welfare' area, with a couple of large tables, a few chairs and a large boiler for tea making at break times. There were a few very old cast iron radiators scattered around the place, but they had little effect, and the workshop was usually very cold. Well, it wouldn't do to make it too cosy, would it? In the corner of the back section of the workshop there was a small office, which was for use by the chargeman (first line supervisor).

There were several apprentices despatched to 46 shop at this time; Mick Moad, Paul Kenyon, Aubrey Snipe, Clive Akers and me, so I was expecting some lively company over the next few months, and was not disappointed. Some older apprentices were already there, including Ron Walters, John Smith, Herbie Anders and Roy Mulford.

I was allocated to work with a skipper called Charlie Flogdale, another of the larger-than-life characters who were almost commonplace in the dockyard at that time. Charlie was of average height, had a good head of wavy hair and always looked as if he had just shaved. He was known as the 'Gentleman Fitter' by some of his bitter companions, mainly because of his tendency to wear gloves (he hated getting his hands dirty), and to try to keep himself as clean as possible. I wouldn't say Charlie was scared of hard work, but as he himself would say, he had tried it once and didn't like it!

Charlie had a very useful backup income selling TVs and watches. When we had little work we would walk around the southern end of the dockyard and invariably bump into someone Charlie knew. In no time at all he would ask if they wanted a marvellous new watch and pull up his sleeve to display five or six gleaming beauties. If they were interested, the haggling would start, but Charlie didn't give much away.

One of Charlie's favourite walks was to see an old friend of his named Jack Rolf. Jack 'lived' in a small hut on the sea wall near no. 7 Slip; we would visit quite often as it was usually nice and warm, and there was the occasional cup of tea thrown in. Once or twice when we got back to 46 shop the chargeman was waiting for us demanding an explanation as to where we had been. Charlie always claimed that we had been to the stores in search of some 'backnuts', so this then became our code for a walk to see Jack. We did do some work, though.

The first ship we went on, a coastal minesweeper, was a major disappointment. As we were preparing to do some maintenance and repair on its diesel generators, we learned that there had apparently been a cock-up somewhere and these diesels were under contract for repairs by the manufacturer, so we were told not to touch them. Charlie was not best pleased. He had a blazing row (one of many) with the chargeman, who was in any event unable to alter the situation. I'm not sure this helped us to get any good jobs for several weeks afterwards.

Work was fairly patchy, until one day a Lister truck and trailer pulled into the workshop piled high with recently galvanized large bore pipes. The chargeman allocated the job to Mick Moad and me. We were to face up the flanges and install the new pipes into the submarine now in No. 4 Dock. This seemed to be a never-ending job, for as soon as we made progress with this huge mound of pipes another load would be delivered. This was another of those jobs which, although quite important, was very boring. Eventually we had sufficient pipes prepared for installation back into the submarine.

Some of these pipes had to fitted into the submarine's compensation tanks, a job from hell! These large tanks are fitted to the sides of the sub outside the pressure hull. They are normally full of fuel oil, water or a mix of both. Even when they have been emptied and cleaned, for work to be done inside they stink to high heaven as a heavy residue of the oil (which is like a dark mustard slime and stinks of sulphur) cannot be completely removed, and the ventilation is inadequate.

The only entrance or exit from these tanks is via a manhole cover, oval in shape and approximately 18' (less than 50 cm) at its largest point. After half an hour in these tanks you had to get out into the fresh air to clear your head. This in itself was a difficult exercise, almost as if the submarine was giving birth! A couple of wandering leads were all the light available, and these were only permitted once the tanks had been subject to a 'gas free' test, to ensure that all the explosive gases inside the tanks had been extracted.

When we came out of these tanks our coveralls were almost completely covered with this filthy slime, and they would need changing after one day's work. Some of the other pipes were for deck fittings, so we finished the tank work as soon as possible to start these.

Mick Moad and I were still working as a pair. One particularly sunny morning we were working up on the deck and Mick was telling me all about the great film he had seen the previous night, *Mutiny on the Bounty*. He enjoyed the film but was particularly impressed when he read that during the shooting

Marlon Brando had taken a shine to one of the leading ladies (a Tahitian beauty), and disappeared into the jungle with her for 'dirty dirties' lasting for several weeks!

We were on deck in the sunshine, filing our flanges, but Mick was obviously unhappy about something. Suddenly he asked 'How many weeks' leave do we get in the year?' Slightly puzzled, I replied 'Two weeks Mick, you know that'.

All quiet. Then he said, more to himself than to me, 'That means I'll have to work for fifty weeks to get two weeks off'. Then he went on 'That means I will have to work for a hundred years to get two years off! Sod that, I'm off to throw a few bolts at the jellyfish.' (At the head of the dock was the caisson and the sea wall ran alongside; often when we walked along here we could see jellyfish and the odd eel.) So off he went, and that's what he did. We didn't see him any more that day.

Some of the other characters working at 46 shop were quite strange in their own right. One of the senior fitters, Bill, must have been in his middle sixties and had health problems. He also had a thing about fire. Often when you were filing away at one end of a long pipe, you could suddenly smell smoke, and looking at the other end you would see Bill poking a ball of smouldering rag into the pipe end and chuckling to his heart's content. This wasn't the only place he left his 'toys', for he would put them under your seat or anywhere else as the occasion arose. Pyromaniac or what?

Another oddball was Ambrose. He was short and fat and usually quiet until going-home time. He would then make a big display of stripping off his coveralls and making sure his trousers were pulled down to his knees, revealing a pair of bright red silk underpants. He would strut around in his little area, posing and clutching his genitals, asking any apprentices present 'Do you want some of this? This is the real stuff'. We all thought this was highly amusing for the first week, but it soon became boring, as the routine was never varied. All the same we all made sure that we weren't caught alone with him in one of the confined spaces on board ship, just in case he really was a queer.

One Friday payday Charlie, my skipper, was expecting to be paid some allowances for working in filthy conditions (obnoxious conditions money). The amount would vary depending on how many hours you worked in those conditions but would usually be about £1. The other fitters on the gang drew their money and received the normal £1, but Charlie was paid just 1s 3d, and he was not amused. He stormed into the chargeman's office and demanded an explanation. He was told that as he had spent so little time on the ship, this was all he was due. He told the chargeman that the only people who received any extra money were his favourites, and he could poke his 1s 3d up his arse! With that he threw his pay packet across the workshop, saying 'One and three for working all of the week in all that shit, you must be joking, bloody good job I'm going out tonight to sell a telly!'

I didn't learn a lot while I was working with Charlie, well not about engineering skills, anyway.

Some of the other apprentices in 46 shop were working for

the Weapons Section rather than for 'our' engine room party, and although we all mingled at dinnertimes etc. we had different supervisors. The chargehand for the weapons team was 'Sarge' Patman. John Patman was an excitable sort of guy at the best of times and could change his moods quite dramatically, especially if the subject of the war came up. One day at afternoon tea break, Sarge was talking to a group of lads across the workshop from us and as usual Paul Kenyon was twittering away taking the piss in the background. Sarge heard most of the comments and ignored them, until Paul said something like 'I bet you were a real hero in the war, Sarge, fighting all those Jerries'.

Sarge snapped. Face scarlet, eyes bulging, he grabbed a broom and shoved it handle-first into Paul's stomach. 'Yes!' yelled Sarge, 'and this is how we used to bayonet the bastards!' With this he thrust the broom handle at Paul again and again until he was backed up against the far wall. Paul went white, and I'm sure he thought that his time had come. However Sarge gave him a couple more good digs with the broom handle, and then, muttering 'Yes, that's the way we did it', he stormed off. Paul was quiet and very selective with his piss taking for the rest of the day!

The work supply was very patchy, and without any work to do we apprentices soon got bored. One day, for some reason or other, we decided to re-enact the burial-at-sea ritual, the burial party consisting mainly of Mick Moad, Paul Kenyon and me. Mick and I laid Paul on the large mess table, crossed his hands, put large washers over his eyes and draped a large union jack (I don't know where we got that from) over him. We said a few solemn words and then lifted one end of the table very, very slowly so that Paul slid down onto the floor. One of the other apprentices was at the same time doing a very good impersonation of a bosun's whistle, just like the real thing. We had not seen the chargeman approaching; as Paul slid on to the floor and we all collapsed laughing, we noticed him standing in the doorway with a totally bewildered expression on his face. We tidied up hurriedly, expecting a major bollocking, but the chargeman never mentioned the escapade. I did notice that after that he often looked at us as if he was optimistically searching for a glimmer of sanity.

Funny how some silly things remain in our memories. One such incident was when one of the fitters had unfortunately died and his tools were going to be sold off, proceeds to the widow. Instead of pricing and selling the toolbox contents individually, which was the traditional way of doing things, it was decided to ask for bids for the complete toolbox, locked up and contents unseen. Most of us put in bids, as was the custom, but one of the lads who had more money than the rest of us put in a high bid and made sure that we knew about it. In fact he gloated. He duly won the prize, and tried to open the toolbox without us seeing. Some chance.

The toolbox was almost full of wooden file handles, worth only a few pence each, and a few worn and inexpensive tools. Did we ever give him a hard time! 'This is the guy that bought a toolbox full of file handles, ha ha ha!' Was the expression 'buying a pig in a poke' ever better demonstrated?

Mick Moad and Paul Kenyon had become great pals, and decided that they would go to Spain for their week's holiday. I think Mick had a somewhat calming influence on Paul, so at least they did not get into any major trouble. However Mick told us about one episode which had us in stitches.

Mick had left Paul in a bar on this night and gone back to the hotel to catch up on some sleep. He was rudely awakened at about 2 am by loud mutterings and the sound of water running in the bedroom's wash basin. This persisted, so in spite of Mick's attempts to ignore the interruption to his sleep, he raised himself up on one elbow to see what was happening. Paul had his cock in the wash basin, half full of water and the tap running. He was scrubbing away at his organ with Mick's nailbrush.

'What are you doing?' Mick asked.

'Well, that dirty cow didn't smell too fresh, and she looked a bit too pleased after I had turked her' he said. 'You can't be too careful, I don't want to go home with VD.'

Mick didn't want his nailbrush back.

Our social lives had picked up a little now, as we had a little money to spend and we had found youth clubs to go to most nights of the week. These were simple pleasures - a game of table tennis, play a few records and meet up with your friends. Of course the major incentive was that you might meet some girls. The clubs we looked forward to most were Tuesday night, above the Co-op in Rainham High Street, Friday at the Central Hall in Chatham and Saturday in the school hall Rainham. Buddy Holly, Eddie Cochrane and Elvis were played of course. Skin-tight jeans and Old Spice aftershave. Happy days.

It was time to change sections again, and this time I was sent to the Crane Repair Section, on the Yard Services Department. Before you were allowed to start work you were interviewed by the Foreman, and the interview went something like this:

Foreman: 'Are you afraid of working at heights?'

Me: 'I don't know Sir, I haven't done it, but I can't say that I am keen.'

Foreman: 'Well, try it for a couple of weeks, and if you're still worried after that time, come back to see me again'.

This was all standard stuff. Experience had shown that after two weeks most people would be acclimatized to working at heights and although at that stage it was still a little daunting, it did not continue to terrify.

The workshop, to the south of no. 7 slip, was an old converted storehouse where slings and crane wire ropes were kept. It was a single-skinned building with a very high roof space, poor lighting and no heating (the chargeman's office at the far end did have a small electric heater).

The gang comprised the chargeman, Tom Hill, and fitters Fred Choke, Mick Kenny, Alan Howland and Ernie Hayes. Dave Else was the skilled labourer, and there were two apprentices, Dave Campbell (Panda) and myself. There were probably others who I cannot remember.

This 'workshop' was cold, damp and miserable and we ate our dinner sitting huddled on our toolboxes. I was allocated to work with Fred Choke as my skipper. Fred was very smart, probably because he was ex-Army. He always had nicely polished boots and a miserable expression on his face. However we got on reasonably well and were employed on repairing the overhead travelling cranes in the dockyard workshops. All was fine and dandy until, after I had been there about three weeks, my mates came home on leave (one was in the Air Force, the other in the Navy), and we went out on a bender on the Friday night. I excelled myself that night and at last showed my mates that I could drink as well as they could. We ended up in the Viscount Hardinge in Gillingham for our eighth pint!

I had to work overtime the following morning, and for some reason I didn't feel very well. After about an hour at work, feeling like a rabbit having a poop, I crept off and hid in one of the nearby railway trucks to try to get my head down and recover. I could not rest, as it was so bloody cold. I still felt sick, and when I started to doze off I had a recurring nightmare that I had fallen asleep, the train had moved and I would wake up in Portsmouth. I went back to the workshop, still feeling ill, at about 11.45.

Fred was not amused. On Monday I was transferred - no sense of humour there. I went to the other (internal) section, working on dockside cranes. This was in my opinion dangerous work. Climbing up vertical ladders at the side of the cranes was no picnic at any time, but when the ladders were wet or icy and it was blowing hard, it was even less so. It was always worse coming down. The horrible bit was to stand at the top of the ladder, turn backwards and try to find the first rung of the ladder with your foot. And of course we did not climb the ladder empty handed; you always had a bag of tools in one hand, and usually a large grease gun slung over your shoulder.

I remember the first time I went up a crane jib with one of the fitters, Mick Kenny, and halfway up the jib he stopped and asked me if I wanted to grease the bearing halfway up or do the one at the top. I said that I would do the one halfway up, but when he pointed to it I asked 'where's the ladder?' (to access the bearing in the middle of the jib). Mick laughed and said that what was required was to climb across the jib itself to access the bearing. Sod that. I changed my mind and plumped for the bearing at the top - at least I had something to hang on to!

We got extra money for working at heights. It wasn't much but we certainly earned it.

Tom Hill, the chargeman, was Welsh, and a miserable bastard. This probably wasn't all his fault as at that time he was also the Mayor of Chatham, and the word was that after particularly hard nights doing his civic duty he could be a little liverish in the mornings.

My 'tour of duty' on this section was in midwinter, and our best efforts to heat up the workshop were by lighting a fire in a modified five-gallon oil drum in the centre of the workshop. This was commonplace in the older workshops. The apprentice's job last thing before going home was to go and pinch some coal from one of the many steam cranes in the area for the next morning's fire. One very cold day most of us were reluctant to leave the comparative warmth of the workshop, and Tom Hill was obviously in a bad mood. When he came out of his office shortly after start time, he told us to get out and on the job, glared around at all and sundry and returned to his office. Most of us stirred, pulled on our heavy fearnought jackets and prepared to leave. Incidentally these fearnought jackets were great at keeping out the cold, as they were manufactured from a duffel coat or blanket type of material, but they were rubbish when they got wet, as they just soaked up the water and were very difficult to get dry again.

Dave, the other apprentice on the gang, was heating a tin of soup on the fire and was a little behind the rest of us with his preparations to leave. Within a few minutes Tom came out of his office again, in an obvious rage, and glared at the apprentice. 'I told you to get out and start work!' he shouted, and gave the tin of soup a hearty kick. It ended up halfway down the workshop, leaving a trail of tomato in its wake. Yes, Tom could have his moments.

He upset my skipper, Alan Howland, and me one day. We had just got to work and it had started to snow really hard. The job we were working on was a steam rail gauge crane at the dockyard main locks entrance, at the farthest end of the yard. We knew the dockyard bus service was due to pass the workshop within the next fifteen minutes or so, which meant that we could wait fifteen minutes in comparative warmth, catch the bus and still arrive at our workplace at the same time or earlier than if we had walked. When we suggested this to Tom he went mad and told us to get out and start walking. This meant we walked the two miles to the locks where we were to work in four inches of snow, which was coming over the top of our boots, in a bitterly cold snow storm.

Well, we did just that. We had little choice. But by the time we had got to the crane we were working on and swept most of the snow off, it was time to head back to the workshop for the mid-morning tea break!

In spite of the fact that it was hard, cold, and sometimes quite dangerous on this section I enjoyed this period of my apprenticeship, and thinking of it still makes me smile.

Our social lives had by now improved a great deal, as we were now earning slightly above desperation wages, and we all had girlfriends. One of my close mates, Dave 'Panda' Campbell, was a good-looking swine who could charm the birds from the trees. He used to travel home to Dover at the weekends and we could not wait until Monday morning when he would relay all the sordid details of his fantastic weekends.

There were always dances, and some quite well-known bands played at the Strand Palais (Deal), Leas Cliff Halls (Folkestone) or the Town Hall in Dover. I'm sure some of the escapades he related to us were to say the least highly exaggerated, and of course they became even more so as they were retold among us apprentices. If he had a fight involving two of his mates and himself against three soldiers, by the time the story had been told a few times it became Dave and two of his mates against ten marine commandos, yet Dave's side nearly always won.

One of the classic interludes was when on one Monday

morning Dave came to work almost unable to walk. He was creeping about like an old man of eighty. Unusually, we had some difficulty prising information about the events which had led up to this situation from him, but not for long.

It seemed Dave and mates had been to the local 'hop' and he had ended up having the last few dances with one of the local beauties. He had secured a promise that he could walk her home. They had of course stopped halfway, and he had tried his best make her go all the way. After much heaving and grunting she had offered to 'help him out', as he had persistently put her hand on his rampant penis. She offered the 'hand shandy' alternative to full sex. Dave said that she was terrific and was giving him the wank of a lifetime when the large dress ring she was wearing turned around on her finger and began cutting into the head of his cock on each downward stroke. He was in agony, but his pained mutterings were only mistaken for indications of ecstasy.

Dave said 'It hurt like hell, but I could not tell her to stop'. Well, it certainly made us stop. We were helpless with laughter, and by the time he got to the punchline we were paralytic.

Dave really made the most of the fact that he had to stay in Medway all the week for work and then travel home to Dover at weekends, as this gave him the chance to have a girlfriend at each end. When he first started courting his long-term girlfriend at Dover he had an older girlfriend who worked in a hotel in Rochester. She would arrange for him to stay overnight at this hotel when the opportunity arose. I think he thought he had won the pools, and boy were we all jealous! Mind you it did cause him some major problems at the later stages, trying to keep the two of them unknown to each other, and the usual difficulties associated with this kind of arrangement.

Paddy and I had also got ourselves girlfriends by this time. Paddy had just started courting a girl called Barbara Kember who was one of the regulars at a local youth club, and lived fairly near to me in Rainham. Paddy used to cycle up to my house and leave his bike there. We would go out for the evening and when we returned he would cycle home. I don't think his first date was a roaring success, as when he came back to collect his bike he had a worried look on his face.

'What's up with you?' I asked. He was reluctant to answer, but eventually he looked me in the eye and asked: 'Which way do you snog, Nige?' I was at first worried, then baffled.

'What do you mean?' I ventured.

'Well,' he said, 'When I went to kiss her goodnight she went like this'. He cocked his head to one side, putting on a passable impression of a pout. 'I did the same, but our noses clashed and she ended up with a nosebleed!'

In spite of the severity of his plight I could not answer - I was helpless with the giggles. I think he sorted out that particular problem in quick time, and without my help.

At that time he must have been very fond of the name Barbara, as he had been seeing another one, Barbara Webb, for a few dates some time previously. Sadly, at about this time she was killed when she fell from a carnival float while parading as the Upchurch Carnival Queen. Although Paddy had not been courting her for long, it really upset him.

For my part I was courting a girl called Larry. I had been out with her for a few months the year previously when she had lived in Strood, but for some reason it had petered out, although we kept in touch.

We got back together again after I had been on a night out with the boys. We had been to several pubs in Chatham, and after closing time my nephew Richard (Dood) and I decided that we would walk home via Bob Webb's home in Luton. After we left Bob it occurred to me that Larry lived just around the corner and it would be rude not to visit, wouldn't it?

So we knocked. Larry and her mum were still both up and happy to let us in. Larry's mum was very tolerant and even seemed slightly amused to see us, and she offered us a cup of tea. Larry discovered that they had run out of milk, so to cut a long story short, Larry and I headed off to a vending machine in the next street. We got the carton of milk and nearly made it all the way back to her house, but unfortunately next to her house was a dark alley. We had a little peck at the entrance and that lit the blue touchpaper. We almost fell into the alley and went straight into a frantic snogging session.

Larry was doing her best to hold on to the milk, but it was becoming very difficult, and in the end she dropped it. I was randy as hell. Fired up with a belly full of beer, which always did it for me, I was as hard as a stone goat. I had three fingers inside Larry, and she was making progressively louder cooing noises: I was about to go for greatest shag of all time when the back door, just the other side of the fence, opened and Larry's mum came out, talking to herself.

Most of the alley was illuminated. That killed the moment. We went in and had our cup of tea, but I was never sure if my dirty fingers had made the milk smell funny, or if I had managed to get the smile off my face.

I was courting Larry for some months afterwards. She was really considerate. She was never content to send me home with a goodnight kiss but always insisted on giving me a good wank to 'make sure I would behave myself until I saw her again'. Who was I to argue?

I was now nearing the end of my fourth year of apprenticeship. The last section I was sent to was Fitters Afloat 1 (FA1). The fitters afloat gangs, as the name implies, work mainly on board naval ships rather than in the workshops. Their work involves the repair and replacement of all the equipment fitted to these ships.

If you have never worked on board one of the Navy's ships - DON'T. The working conditions were primitive. When a ship was called in for refit it had to run on temporary supplies from shore, and this invariably meant that there would be no heating and very poor lighting aboard. Believe me, even if a ship is not surrounded by water, ie it was in dry dock, it is unbelievably cold in the winter months. Not surprising really, when you consider that everywhere you are surrounded by cold metal. Next is the noise; the power tools used by the various trades, chipping hammers, paint-removing 'knobblers', pneumatic wrenches and other assorted hand and power tools. Deafening Jet Vac pumps were used to remove bilge water.

Welding was going on everywhere, so while you were shielding your eyes from the welding flashes you would hit your head on some overhead obstruction, or fall down a hole, or both.

Apart from welding, specialist paints, gas–cutting metals and running machinery, the fumes were probably the worst. And asbestos was everywhere. Very little care was taken to minimize exposure to this, in fact it was treated in a very cavalier way, with people throwing it about all over the place!

Everything was either wet or damp. Combine this with oil/diesel/antifreeze residue and you end up with a surface like an ice rink. The lighting provided by wandering leads was generally very poor, and as a lot of the work was undertaken in very confined spaces, it was particularly nasty in the bowels of the ship. As you can probably tell, I didn't think working under these conditions was much fun!

At this time health and safety education and implementation in Chatham Dockyard was in its infancy. Compartments on board ship were not cleared when lagging (asbestos) was being removed. Ear defenders were not available to everyone, and the effect of toxic fumes was not fully understood, or it was ignored. In fact there was a culture that it was unmanly to request any safety equipment, probably the only exception being the wearing of safety goggles, as so many workmen had lost eyes. A cynical view would be that the overriding priority of the Navy Department was to complete the ship's refit on time, sometimes to the detriment of the health and safety of the workforce.

The FA1 workshop was on the north side of No. 2 Basin, behind the Navy's MTE (Maintenance Training Establishment) workshop. I was allocated to work with my skipper, Johnny Wicks. Apparently when I first arrived in the workshop, to disguise my apprehension and nervousness I stormed up to the nearest fitter and demanded 'Where's this bloke Wicks?' No wonder they thought 'we've got a right one here'!

The rest of the gang were decent sorts. The fitters tended to work in pairs, the two main couples being Sam Legg and Alan Lewis, and Barry Obie and Paddy Banks. The chargeman on this gang was Charlie Carpenter, a great guy. He took the apprentices under his wing and treated them very fairly, with a good understanding that we were young, inexperienced and high spirited. Even a pain in the arse like me!

Johnny Wicks likewise was a gem. He would always take the time to explain things, and we became great mates. One problem with working with John though was that his timekeeping was little better than mine!

The works recorder on this section was a guy called Ray Turner, who drove a little 1939 Standard Flying 9 which had once been blue and had seen better days. It used to look funny when it was driven over the railway line on the caissons, as the wheels would wobble dramatically, but somehow it had a character all of its own.

I had seen a similar one for sale in a garage in Rainham and liked it, so I pestered Ray to sell me his, which he eventually did. My first car - it cost me £5. This was a bargain that I was happy with, although there were a few jobs which needed doing.

My brother-in-law Derek, who was a qualified driver and a mechanic, went with me to collect the little car and drove it home for me to the garage I had rented. He commented 'It drives and pulls quite well', to which I replied, 'Yes, but perhaps we ought to release the handbrake!' It obviously didn't work too well.

Over the next couple of weeks Derek fully checked the car over and did the repairs necessary to make it reasonably safe and reliable. The major repairs necessary were replacement suspension pins (this would stop the excessive wheel wobble), a new steering nut (this would only last six months as the mating part in the steering rack was badly worn as well), a new clutch plate, a pair of pre-focus headlights and from the local scrap yard a pair of part-worn tyres, on their wheels.

One incident regarding this little car will stay in my memory for all time. One Sunday afternoon my girlfriend Larry had come up to see how the repairs were progressing, and seemed reasonably impressed with what had been done in such a short time. She was a little cracker (Larry, not the car), and I was a normal teenager with a rampant sex drive. To cut a long story short we ended up in the back seat of the Standard enjoying a very intense lovemaking session. I was quite nervous because the car was up on jacks, and as we changed position on the back seat of the car some worrying noises could be heard as the jacks moved. To be honest by that time I would not have cared if the car had fallen off of a cliff face, let alone the jacks!

This was the first time I discovered the delights of the 69

position, a truly unforgettable experience, in the back seat of a 1939 Flying 9 and up on jacks!

My mate Paddy Hargan helped me to sand down and repaint the car over the Easter holiday. I now had a colour choice and settled for a two-tone finish, red on the bottom, cream on top. We worked really hard on the car and although it was hand-painted rather than sprayed, it looked really smart when finished.

To celebrate the finish of the repairs we agreed to take her out for a trial run, and decided we would go to Whitstable. We had a full load on board, Derek alongside me in the front and Mum, sister Chris and baby Mark in the back seat. All went well; the car was running nicely, and there was no sign of problems until we got a few miles along the Thanet Way and were stopped by a police motorcyclist. My (applied for) road tax disc had not come back from the issuing body, so I would be prosecuted, a good start to my motoring career!

As he had stopped us the copper decided to check over the car, and proceeded to each corner, pushing down hard on the wings to test the suspension. Mark started crying, so the policeman stopped and asked what was wrong. My sister had the presence of mind to say 'It's the uniform, officer, it frightens him, I'm sorry'. The policeman showed his caring side and discontinued the car's examination, told me that I would be prosecuted for not displaying a tax disc and left.

Further down the road, a little puzzled, I asked Chris 'How long has the baby been like that, with a thing about uniforms?'

'He hasn't' she replied. 'But when the policeman was

rocking the suspension, something was pushing the seat and him up and down from beneath and that's what frightened him!'

I needed a qualified driver to accompany me until I passed my test. As John Wicks lived near me it was agreed that he would call for me in the mornings, leave his pushbike at my house and come to work with me in my 'new' car. This was great in theory; the only trouble was that John was almost as bad as I was at getting up in the mornings. If I wasn't late he was, and vice versa. In the end the pair of us were late so often that we were both on prompt muster. The rest of the gang thought this was hilarious, and probably the first time in the dockyard's history that a skipper and his apprentice were put on prompt muster together. What fame!

However, this seemed to sort us out, and from that time on both of us mended our ways and achieved normal attendance records.

I think Johnny Wicks was nearly as fond of the little Standard as I was. His favourite expression was that the car had 'semi elliptic laminated transverse leaf springing' - it took me some time to work out that this meant that it had bloody great springs at the back. It also had cable brakes, six-volt ignition, no radio, no heater and a three-speed gearbox. It made a pronounced squeak when you went around a corner as the suspension was so worn that the tyres would rub against the body, a different sound if you turned left or right! It also had a tendency to slide down a camber if you braked hard on certain roads, so you had to turn the wheel to compensate. It certainly wasn't fast. We would often chase rabbits when driving home from the country pubs we used to frequent, and the rabbits invariably won.

What it did have was a starting handle (thank god), and character - bags and bags of character. I had that car for six months, and then sold it to one of the other apprentices.

At work things were progressing very well. The fitter's afloat gang were in the main a decent gang, so much so that we would occasionally meet up, usually on a Friday night, at the Dewdrop pub for a game of darts. Bob Webb and I used to play a lot of darts at this time and on one of these Fridays we were both playing very well. The convention was that the winners stayed on the board and played the next challengers. This Friday we started at about 8.30 and beat all comers until just before closing time, when we both got bored and fatigue overtook us. The landlord was very impressed with our darts display and almost begged us to join his darts team. We declined, as we had no intention of being tied into this routine. The next time we went to the pub we played really badly, our games were rubbish and the landlord ignored us. Heroes to zeros in two weeks!

The major task for our fitter's gang was the refit of HMS *Rame Head*, and it was here that I first encountered asbestos. In the machinery spaces on board ship it was commonplace, and we thought it hilarious to throw large quantities of asbestos at each other, like a snowball fight. Another party piece, usually by a visiting tradesman, was to give the asbestos pipe covers a hefty blow, which showered the immediate area with a blanket of asbestos dust - what fun!

The exposure to this dust was aggravated by the encouragement to work 'time in lieu', which basically meant that you took half an hour for your lunch and left work half an hour earlier in the evening. The idea was to increase production; the workforce would not go back to 'shore' for their lunch but eat it on board, mostly where they worked, to reduce stoppage time. This meant that many workmen ate their sandwiches in an obnoxious environment, full of asbestos dust!

Another amazing (to me at the time) was the number of toilets required at the side of the dockyard basins to satisfy convention. The Navy had separate 'heads' (as the toilets are termed) for ratings, POs/CPOs and officers, while the dockyard requirement was for separate toilets for workmen, chargemen, inspectors and foremen – four more types, making seven in all. This seemed like severe overkill, but when you visited some of the workmen's toilets and saw what sort of state that they were left in, the picture became a little clearer.

When we finished the refit of the *Rame Head* (a submarine depot ship), a team was selected to go out with her on sea trials, and I was one of them. This in itself was a compliment, as only those who were considered to have contributed significantly to the refit were considered.

The sea trial started for me on a Sunday morning. The trials party had to assemble at Chatham's Bull's Nose (the locks entrance), and we would be taken by trot boat to Sheerness, where the *Rame Head* had anchored, having left Chatham Dockyard on Friday previously.

When she left on Friday most of us were a little jealous that an advance party, which included some of the workmen who lived furthest away, would be going with her and would therefore be entitled to two days' extra pay. In the event the fitters' team on board earned their extra money, as a minor problem arose on an important piece of equipment (the manoeuvring valve), and a considerable effort was required in the short time available to ensure that the ship was ready to start her sea trials proper on Monday.

The first day on board was one of familiarization. Although I knew the ship from the period I had spent working on her, it seemed very different now with almost all the machinery running. Another difference was that all the ship's crew were aboard now, running the ship's machinery, discussing the trials programme details and taking readings from all the active equipment.

Most of the compartments were fairly crowded at this time as the Navy and civilians were working in tandem running, checking, adjusting and handing over equipment. It was noisy, hot and crowded. The apprentices were told to make themselves scarce for a while until the initial activities were all set in place, as generally space was at a premium and we were going to get in the way. We headed for the Mess area and enjoyed ourselves playing cards and darts.

Charlie Carpenter, our chargeman, came around to check on us later in the afternoon, and I took the opportunity to plead with him to let me join the refit party in the main engine room. He was a little hesitant, but I finally persuaded him with the argument that this was a one-off opportunity for me to gain some first-hand experience on this variety of operational equipment, and that I was keen as mustard to help. Persuaded by my enthusiasm, he instructed me to report to him in the engine room, after the initial early morning checks, not before 10 o'clock.

At 10 o' clock I entered the engine room at deck level and made my way down the first two vertical ladders, working my way down the interim levels to approach the engine room landing. As I got halfway down the final ladder, about five feet from the grating, a fuel oil pipe above my head burst. It was not a major burst, a joint had failed, but it was enough to frighten the life out of me and soak me through with warm oil with the consistency of treacle. I stood there shocked, doing an impression of Nat King Cole and wondering quite what to do next.

That problem was solved for me. Charlie came storming over from the opposite side of the platform, looked at me in disgust, and said 'You, you must be a Jonah, fuck off!'

I could not believe my bad luck. I was distraught beyond words, but could do nothing except sneak off for a shower and change of clothes. I thought it best not to pester Charlie for another job too much for the rest of that day, but next morning I felt sufficiently confident to try again.

Charlie had a sympathetic smile on his face next morning, and asked how I was. I decided that this was a good time to ask for another job and was surprised when he said that he had just the thing for me. He said one of the main shaft plumber blocks was showing a tendency to overheat, so my job would be to monitor it.

The good news was that I had been given another job to do;

but the bad news was, what were these plumber blocks, and where were they?

It all became clear very soon. Charlie took me right down to the shaft tunnel at the bottom of the ship. The shaft tunnel is the very long compartment which carries the main drive shaft along the bottom of the ship and out through the stern gland into the water. There it is connected to the propeller which drives the ship.

At frequent intervals, about twenty feet apart, are large bearings which support the shaft, housed in casings called plumber blocks. My job was to monitor the temperature of these bearings by placing my hand on to the top of the blocks, feeling for any sharp increase in temperature: not very scientific, but I was told that if I checked these bearings in this way at intervals of say fifteen minutes, it would be an effective and vital check.

The shaft tunnel was, in common with most other ships' compartments, very poorly lit. The headroom was such that I could not stand upright, so in making frequent journeys along the tunnel to check these bearings I must have looked like Quasimodo on a bad day. Worse still, I was not wearing my watch (it was still covered with oil residue), and had no idea of the time. I came out of the tunnel a couple of times and made my way up to the engine room to check the time, convinced that I had been down there for at least three hours, only to find out that it was only an hour and a quarter since I had started my checks. Time certainly dragged, and it was easy for my imagination to run riot.

After a few forward and back checks I decided to have a look at the stern gland, where the propeller shaft exited the ship. It was leaking! I decided that this needed to be reported immediately, before we all sank, and trying to disguise my panic I went back to report the revelation to Charlie Carpenter. He did me the courtesy of coming back with me to investigate, and then explained that the water leaking passed the gland which had caused me such alarm was in fact the means of cooling the bearing, and perfectly normal. I just wished someone had told me earlier.

When I returned to my place of duty back inside the shaft tunnel, I had another quick look at the stern gland, just to make sure. It was then that it occurred to me that the spot where I was working was about fifteen feet below the water line. Bloody hell! What if we hit an iceberg? I would be the last one out. By the time I had got halfway up all the ladders to get to the deck, I would be in Davy Jones' locker. I controlled my panic and resumed my routine checks as instructed, but it just shows how the imagination can cause havoc in a confined, dark space when you are on your own.

After two days doing the checks in the shaft tunnel, Charlie decided that the bearings no longer presented a threat and that I could come up from my isolation and join the others. Looking back I'm not sure if this job was as urgent as it was supposed to be, or if it was a convenient means of keeping me out of the way, just in case I was a Jonah!

The rest of the trial went really well. The Navy were very

happy to accept the ship, as all equipment had been tested and operated well within the required limits. We got back into Chatham mid-afternoon on Friday.

A couple of weeks later the eagerly-awaited 'trials pay' was in our pay packets, and it was by far the biggest sum that I had received in wages since starting work. I don't remember the amount, but I do remember that it included overtime and several trials allowances, and at that time I believe it was comparable to over three weeks' normal pay.

That was the good news. Unfortunately, shortly afterwards, my girlfriend Larry decided that she and I were finished. She was already seeing someone else. She didn't even tell me - it was just that each time I called for her she was late getting home, or not there, so it just petered out.

The last time I called to take her out was a little frightening, but looking back it was probably one of my biggest opportunities lost. I called as usual to find Larry out, so her mum let me in. She said she thought her daughter would not be long and that she would make us a cup of tea while I waited for her.

When she came back with the tea she came and sat down beside me on the settee; looking back, that was unusual. After we had drunk our tea, with still no sign of Larry, I asked her mum if she knew where she had gone. She talked vaguely about a place I had never heard of in Gillingham, but as I asked her where it was she suddenly put her hand on my thigh. She then proceeded to draw a map of the location, travelling up, down and inside my tensed thigh, while I squirmed and did my utmost to disguise the onset of a serious stiffy.

I confess that I chickened out, mumbled farewell and left. Her actions did not seem quite blatant enough for me to be 100% sure that we were replaying that scene from *The Graduate* - but who am I kidding, of course we were. I rather regret that I did not have the balls to take her up on it. If she was anything like her daughter it would have been a fantastic experience! Sadly, I will never know.

The sea trials were almost at the end of my period of training on the afloat section, where I learned how all the support functions for the ship's refit came together and saw how things worked at the sharp end. It also marked the end of my fourth year of apprentice training.

CHAPTER 5

FINAL YEAR

When my apprentice entry finished our fourth year of training, we were all sent into the factory to compensate for the acute shortage of skilled machinists.

The foreman interviewed each of us individually to explain this unusual occurrence, and to discuss any preference we had concerning which section we would like to work on.

The interview was quite short, as he had about thirty lads to see, but it could be paraphrased in my case as:

Foreman: 'OK Mr Smith, tell me where you would like to work, and I'll see if I can match your choice to my requirements.'

Me: 'Thank you sir. I would like to work on the diesels section.'

Foreman: 'Sorry, report to the heavy turning section.'

Most of the apprentices told a similar story. There was a desperate need for machinists, so that was where we were going. *Fait accompli.*

The heavy turning section was where large, heavy-duty capstan lathes were operated. The capstan lathe had a turret pre-loaded with the required tools for a specific job. It was fairly quick in operation and generally used to produce high numbers in batch work.

The chargeman of the section showed me to my allocated lathe and left me with instructions to familiarize myself with the operation of it and practise on a few dummy workpieces, as I would not be given a job proper until the following day. The next day I practised some more on the lathe and had a chance to scrutinize the other workmen on the section. This worried me a great deal. Because the work was almost entirely on the bonus scheme, the men worked their socks off to earn the big bucks. That in itself was OK, but because of the repetitive nature of the jobs the men were like zombies, jumping up to start work as soon as the hooter (start of work signal) went, then watching a machine do a repeat operation for perhaps a thousand cycles, stopping only for dinner and the odd toilet break before starting again. No wonder they looked like lost and depressed souls.

Around mid morning the chargeman came to see me, and asked how I was getting on. He didn't seem impressed when I could not display the enthusiasm he was looking for. He told me that my first job had been delayed, but would be delivered before dinnertime. He also said that it would be a good job for me to start on - it was five thousand flanges for HMS Forth.

I thought that at least he had a sense of humour. Five thousand flanges, that's a good one!

Guess what happened, just before dinner? A Lister truck arrived at my lathe, complete with a trailer behind, both loaded to overflowing with blank flanges - all for me.

The work required on these flanges was to face, drill, bore and cut a welding radius. The flanges had been flame-cut in the boiler shop, which had the effect of hardening the material around the cuts. This meant that hardened (tipped) tools had to be used to cut them, and a lubricant/coolant cutting fluid needed to be sprayed continuously while cutting was being done.

I mention the above details to give an insight into the working environment. You had to start work as soon as the hooter went. Every time the lathe cutting tool hit the flange it produced a high-pitched screaming noise while cutting the hardened flanges, and the lubricant/coolant splashed back on to your face and hands. To say I wasn't keen would be something of an understatement.

The chargeman came back in the afternoon and tried to cheer me up by telling me that if I worked hard and did well I might be considered for overtime. Bloody hell! I didn't like the idea of eight hours a day doing this work, and no way was I going to ask for overtime.

I looked at one of the 'top men' on the section, a ginger-haired guy aged about thirty. His job was to manufacture catapult breaking rings, which were (a) manufactured to very exact requirements, and (b) required on a continuous basis. This guy looked ancient before his time, at least ten years older than his actual age, suffered permanent styes around his eyes and had a grey, defeated appearance. Any interest and enthusiasm he might once have had for anything other than work had been drowned by the necessity to work continuously for up to 60 hours a week on a repetitive task.

Later in the week I had a visit from Paul 'the mad' Kenyon,

who was now working in the factory as well. I was having a supermoan about hating the section I was working on and the fact that the need to regularly change the chuck (a heavy drive component on the lathe) was causing me considerable grief, as I had a back problem.

It was then that we hatched our cunning plan. Paul persuaded me that if I went to my doctors and complained about my back, I would be put on sick leave. I didn't need much persuading, especially as he said that he intended to go sick himself next week, and I really hated operating that lathe. He then explained that to make this ruse plausible it would be wise to do a little play-acting. I would need to be seen changing the heavy chuck, and halfway through the operation, I should give a shout of pain and drop the chuck. We did a mini rehearsal, and then, feeling that the moment was right, I went for it.

Bugger me, at the critical time when the nearest spectator should have seen this masterpiece enacted, he was distracted and missed it! I had to repeat the exercise, after a little rest, a short time later. I felt a little guilty about going sick in this way, but in fairness I did have a back problem at this time which certainly was made worse by the heavy lifting on this section, so I exaggerated rather than invented the problem.

I managed to escape from the heavy turning section after continued pleas, and only limited success in my work output; I just could not settle on that section at all. I was transferred to Section 31, Turbines and Auxiliaries, where I would complete my apprenticeship.

The Turbines section comprised about ten fitters and usually a couple of apprentices. When I first joined I thought it would be sensible to get a good understanding of what went on, as I was due to complete my apprenticeship there, and usually you could expect to stay on the section where you completed your time - finished your apprenticeship.

The section was typical of most of those in the factory at that time. The majority of the fitters seemed to be very old. Some actually were, while others were simply old before their time. In common with all the other sections, mine had its own hierarchy; obviously apprentices were at the bottom of the food chain and we were soon made aware of these facts of life, or ignored altogether depending on the prevailing mood. The senior fitters had the pick of the work and input into any of the day-to-day decisions and jealously guarded their seniority. Scattered around the work area were hat pegs, and woe betide any interloper who inadvertently used one of the seniors' pegs. They each had their own little station comprising hat peg, toolbox storage and bench space.

Everyone wore hats. The 'cheesecutter' was the most popular, but others preferred the trilby. A lot of the men had two hats, one they wore on the way to work and an old one they changed into once they got there.

We apprentices used to marvel at one of the old boys in particular. He was almost completely bald and obviously very self-conscious about this, so his hat changing ritual was smooth and professional. Shortly after arriving at work he would place himself facing his hat peg with his work cap in his right hand. He would take a quick look round, and then as the left hand snatched the trilby from his head it was replaced immediately by the work cap in his right hand. A very polished manoeuvre, repeated in reverse at going-home time.

Many of the workmen who changed their clothes before going home were those transferred from Sheerness when that dockyard closed. Transport on special buses was made available, free of charge, for three years after the transfer, in an attempt to soften the impact of the redundancy and other problems that this major shutdown caused.

On section 31 the two lead fitters were Bob Weeks and Bob Nicholls, and they specialized in feed pumps, the pumps which supply water to ships' boilers. These two were definitely first in the pecking order, but perhaps this was quite natural as they had been there the longest, and the chargeman knew that when he gave them a job it would always be done well and in time. No problems. The other fitters on the section included Roy Beard, Norman Stanley, John Jarret and several more elderly fitters whose names I never knew, who would not mix with upstart apprentices.

We worked in pairs, and my first pairing was with Norman Stanley. He was a cheerful ex-Navy man, shortish and fattish. I think we worked very well together, most of the time refitting forced lubrication pumps and other miscellaneous equipment as and when. One job I was given at this time which I really enjoyed was the static balancing of (mainly) large pump impellers. This involved rotating the impeller, its shaft supported on knife edges, to identify the areas of imbalance, so that weights could be added or material removed as appropriate to achieve the balance necessary. We also had a dynamic balancing machine available in the factory at this time, but only one operator was fully trained in the operation of it. This caused continual holdups, as his attendance was unreliable due to sick leave. As I was very interested in this work I applied to go on a course and be trained as a deputy for the balancing machine operator, but of course this did not happen; whether it was a lack of training funds or lack of interest by managers I do not know.

One special forced lubrication pump which Norman and I were working on was urgently required, so we were asked to work overtime on a Saturday to speed the refit. Norman – ex-Navy, remember - liked a pint and decided that we should go for a quick one in the lunch break. I would drive, as at this time he did not have a car.

Going for a drink in the dinner hour presented two problems. First we were not really allowed to leave the dockyard, as we only had half an hour for our break. Second, we needed to have an excuse as to where we had been when we came back to work after the liquid lunch. We thought we would probably get away with stretching the half an hour slightly, and Norman solved the second problem by taking one of the large pump bearings we were refurbishing over to the coppersmiths for remetalling, obtaining an assurance that we could collect it straight after dinner.

So we went for our pint or three, and Norman, being either

a diplomat or a firm believer in insurance, took a bottle of beer back with us for the chargeman, just in case. When we got back we parked up, collected the bearing from the coppersmith's workshop and returned to the side entrance to the factory. As we entered we saw at once that the chargeman had spotted us from the other side of the bay and was making his way towards us. Shit! Had he been looking for us?

We tried to appear ultra casual, with just the expected sense of urgency while making our way back to our workbench. Unfortunately Norman, in his panic, his eyes fixed on the approaching chargeman, did not see a wire hawser stretched across the workshop gangway and tripped.

Bollocks! The bearing, newly remetalled and quite valuable, leapt into the air and did three or four somersaults in slow motion. But Norman redeemed himself. Somehow he regained his balance and caught the bearing with all the aplomb of a test cricketer. It took an unbelievable effort to stop myself laughing.

The chargeman did allow himself a little smile and asked where we had been, but he appeared to be reasonably happy with Norman's explanation that we had gone for a quick pint to celebrate something or other; I kept my mouth shut. I heard the chargeman say later that we couldn't really have been drinking or we would not have juggled so well. Norman presented him with his bottle of beer, so everyone was happy.

Norman had started taking driving lessons, and one day, after much hesitation, he asked me if I would take him out, as the competent driver, to supplement his driving school lessons.

Like a fool I said yes. Norman was the worst would-be driver I had ever met. I used to dread the sessions we had together as he would frighten the life out of me. The most difficult bit was to stop trembling at the end of the lesson, and say 'well that wasn't too bad Norman, you're getting there!' without him noticing the teeth marks on the dashboard and the fact that all colour had been drained from me. During those weeks I gained a complete understanding of a *kamikaze* pilot trainer's mindset. I'm not sure that I had anything to do with it, but when the time came for his test he passed! I do not know to this day whether the examiner was drunk, on drugs or insane. Possibly all three.

As was the custom, I was next moved on to work with another of the fitters, Roy Beard. Roy was a dapper little guy, quite mouthy to the apprentices and sometimes sarcastic to the other fitters on the section. He came from Sheerness, and was a piss-taker extraordinaire. The other thing you would notice about Roy was that he had a glass eye. When I first worked with him I felt a little self-conscious looking at it, but by the end of the first week I felt comfortable enough to ask him how he had lost it.

He explained that he used to work afloat with his mate Stan, who was also at Chatham but on a different section, in the dockyard at Sheerness. Stan and Roy were great mates. One day while chipping off nuts (breaking up nuts which had become impossible to undo due to exposure to extreme temperature) Stan had a splinter fly into his eye, which damaged it beyond treatment. When Stan returned to work complete with glass eye,

Roy suggested that the gang should adopt the usual approach and take the piss, as this would actually help Stan come to terms with his misfortune much more quickly.

So Roy took the piss, and he was good at it. But six months later he suffered an almost identical accident, and lost an eye in the same way. This type of accident was fairly commonplace in the dockyards at that time. Roy was quite happy about his disability, and it affected him very little except that he obviously had no peripheral vision on one side. He said that one of the most embarrassing moments of the whole episode was when he had to go into hospital for an 'eye fitting'. This meant he had to sit on a stool facing a very attractive young female doctor who was looking deeply into his eye for an extended period. This was the medical person whose job it was to match the false eye, colour and pattern, to the existing one!

Although Roy was not top dog on the section, he was sufficiently up the pecking order to get a good selection and variety of jobs. This was good news for me, as working with him I was earning a little bonus pay and expanding my experience on these types of equipment in particular and fitting in general. I got on well with Roy and even used to meet up with him on some Friday nights when with a few mates we ventured into Sheerness. There were some good pubs on the island of Sheppey at that time, and it was always a good night out.

One Friday night we had visited a few pubs in the High Street and the Conservative Club, and decided on fish and chips before we headed home. We scoffed them walking back to the car, and one of the guys with me, inspired by the football on the TV, screwed his wrapper up and threw it at me, calling 'Go on Nige, score with this one.'

I duly obliged, swung my leg to give the 'ball' a hefty swipe - and watched in horror as my winklepicker shot into the air and landed on the first floor windowsill above a shop. It had started to rain and the pavement was wet. I had to knock several times before the door to the flat above the shop was answered, and then had difficulty explaining how my shoe had ended up on this guy's windowsill. In the end he made some comment like 'bloody nutters' and disappeared inside. Seconds later he opened the window, with difficulty, and threw down my shoe. He was not a happy teddy.

The social scene was pretty good at this time. I had recently got myself another car, a beautiful 1957 Wolseley Model 15/50. This cost me £315 from Russell's garage in Rochester, and for that I got gleaming black bodywork, a walnut dash, red leather upholstery and a great chance to impress the birds.

One of our favourite haunts when my mates were home on leave was the Crescendo Club in Chatham, a strip club. It would be very tame by today's standards, but back then it was the dog's bollocks. I'm sure some of the acts were students just earning a few extra pounds in their holidays, although some of the acts mixed in with them were very professional. It was all good clean fun really, as the girls never went completely nude, and the atmosphere was always jovial and friendly.

Except for one night. John 'Stacy' Workman and Jeff Tassell

were a couple of regulars; they used to have a good drink at Rochester Rugby Club and breeze into the Crescendo just before the acts started. When they came in they lit up the place. Always ready with a massive repertoire of jokes, they were noisy and exuberant but never over the top. On this particular Saturday night the boys came in as usual, and sat a few feet away from where me and my mates were sitting. The stripper was doing her act to the strains of *Please don't tease me* by Cliff Richard; the idea was that she would do half of her act while the record played once, then they would play the record again and she would finish it.

All went well until she finished the first part of the act and stopped, bent over and with her bum only just covered with the tiniest pair of knickers, about a foot from Jeff Tassell's nose. He obviously quite enjoyed the scenery, but I believe he was slightly embarrassed, and being always ready with a quip he said 'Charmin', bloody charmin!'

Those of us who knew Jeff realized that this was just a bit of fun, but when several people in the audience started to laugh the girl took it personally. She spun around and snarled at Jeff 'One more remark like that sonny and I'm off'. To which Jeff replied 'Never mind, bring on the dancing girls'.

More laughter, girl storms off. Nothing much happened for several minutes, and no one imagined there was a problem. To cut a long story short, although the boys offered to apologise through the manager, the girl had taken offence and refused to finish her act until they were made to leave. They left, apologizing to the assembled audience but still in high spirits.

The girl came back and finished her act, and when she had finished there was a deathly hush. Not one person clapped. She glowered at us all and stormed off. I don't think she was booked again.

Usually when we left the Crescendo we would have to walk back home to Rainham, so we would often make a slight detour to a coffee stall near the viaduct in Railway Street. This was one of the 'places to be' around midnight on a Friday or Saturday night, as all the local 'celebrities' would call in. Peter Sharp was one of these; a self-proclaimed hard man with a huge mop of fair hair, complete with a DA (duck's arse) haircut of course, and shirt unbuttoned to the waist whatever the weather, he was hard to miss. I must say that I never saw him cause any trouble and he seemed to be a reasonable sort who was just keen on a bit of notoriety.

The major interest at the coffee stall was the motorbikes. I would estimate that there could be over a hundred of them on show on some nights, and what bikes they were!

The main display was in two lines, and they were immaculately-kept models of almost every make. At the top of the range were the Triumph Bonnevilles, Trophies, Model 110s, 100s, Speed Twins etc, Norton Dominators, Model 99s and 88s, BSA Super Rockets, Road Rockets and Gold Stars. Other makes would include Velocette, AJS, Matchless, Triumph Nortons, BSA Nortons and Ariels, while even the odd Vincent Black Shadow or Lightning would appear periodically. One thing most of them had in common was that they were polished to perfection, and were their owners' pride and joy. Many of the owners would admit to taking their bikes into their kitchens to polish up the aluminium engine parts until they gleamed like chromium.

Although I always enjoyed the motorbike show at the coffee stall, it often left me with a nightmare vision of something that I dreamed had happened on one of my occasional visits. I had parked my motorbike on its centre stand and turned away when I heard a crash. My bike had fallen over on to the bike next to it, damaging it and knocking it over. That bike in turn knocked over the one next to it, which resulted in a cascade of damaged motorbikes along the entire line in front of the coffee stall. Shit! I was confronted by 50 snarling bike boys. They were not amused. I was lucky to escape alive.

My preferred fare at the stall was a steak and kidney pie smothered in brown sauce and a cup of tea. Actually, I was not quite sure if it was tea, but it was hot and wet anyway. Thus fortified we could start the trek back to Rainham.

The walk home could be quite eventful. Naturally the task was invariably trying to find somewhere open for more beer, and seek out some women. It was a tall order for young men who were nearly skint, after midnight in the Medway Towns. One plan we would adopt was to head down to Leysdown - there was bound to be some crumpet down there, wasn't there? Fat chance of course, but at the time it always seemed quite feasible. Two occasions when we made attempts spring to mind, but for the time being, as I don't want to chance ending up in jail, they will remain untold!

My next and last move on the Turbines section was to work

with one of the senior hands, Bob Nicholls. Promotion? Perhaps my real potential had been recognized at last! Or it may have been that Bob had lost his regular fitter partner, Bob Weeks, who had been made chargeman when George Allen retired. Anyway, I was now to work with Bob and that suited both of us just fine. Bob was in his sixties, of average build, not much hair left and usually cheerful and chatty.

He was also very nosey. I don't mean that in a nasty way, but he really enjoyed going around the shop floor, mainly on his own section, talking to people and finding out all their business. If you wanted to know anything about anybody, you asked Bob.

The other thing about Bob was that he always LOOKED busy. He always had a small component in one hand, and would polish this intermittently with either a file or a piece of emery paper while he extracted the latest lurid details from all and sundry. You could never say that he was not actually working. He had this game off to a fine art. Having said that, Bob was a nice old guy, harmless and inoffensive. He was also a very good fitter, and would gladly pass on his experience and expertise to anyone who was experiencing technical problems.

When the turbine-driven pumps we were refitting had been completed, they had to be tested. Across the road from the factory was the test house, which had a high pressure steam supply specifically for these tests. We were testing a new to service pump, which meant we would be in the test house for several days. At this time my car was overdue for an oil change, so after agreeing it with Bob I decided that I would do this in one of my dinner-hour breaks while we were working in the test house, a little bit 'out of the way'. The big advantage here was that the car could be driven inside the test house for this work, so even if it was raining it would not present a problem. I had a contact who could get me some high quality oil, so I was all set.

On the day involved we were having problems getting the necessary steam supplies for our test runs, so we started late. In consequence we were a little late taking our dinner break. I started the oil change as soon as I had finished my hurried sandwiches. I had all the old oil drained out and the new oil filter fitted loosely in position, and topped the engine up with the fresh oil.

Of course this was where it all went wrong. Bob, who was keeping watch, suddenly shouted, 'Chargeman's coming Nige, get the car out quick!'

Sure enough the chargeman was on his way over, probably to check if we were having any more problems with the steam supply. Bob went over and operated the roller shutter door, ready for my quick exit. I quickly replaced the oil filler cap, put the tools to one side and reversed the car out. Unfortunately, where the oil filter was not fully tightened, oil was pissing out all over the place. When I checked it later, I found that most of the fresh oil had been wasted. Shit! Still at least we passed inspection by the chargeman and after I had mopped up the oil mess, there were no repercussions. I think I learned several lessons that day.

The time passed quite quickly on this section, and was very interesting, thanks to the variety of jobs that came in. The fitters here were also in the main helpful, and did their best to help us improve and acquire new skills.

I finished my apprenticeship while I was working on this section, and continued there for about another six months. I would probably have been happy to stay there if the work had been more regular, but it was becoming increasingly more patchy with frequent long periods of waiting time with no work to do, as more and more work was being placed with contractors.

At this time a vacancy notice was put on the notice board in the main workshop, asking for applicants for a planning assistant (technical progressman) in the Weapons section. The pay was not great, an allowance of twenty-one shillings a week, but the job sounded interesting and I saw it as an exciting new challenge. I explained to Bob Nicholls that I was thinking of applying for the job, and asked his advice. It was as usual simple and to the point. 'Why not?' he said. 'Go for it old son, there's nothing for you here.'

I applied for the job and got it, so I left the factory and started my new job at the very bottom of the management stream.

And the rest, as they say, is history.

APPENDIX 1

September 1958 Fitter Apprentice Entry

Clive Akers

Jim Apps (BO Apps)

Roy Smith

John Arnold

Clive Walters

Pete Appleby (Ace)

Bob Webb

Malcolm Boorman

Chris Woods

Dave Campbell (Panda)

Vic Salmon

Derek Chambers

Dick Seamark

Alan Clatworthy

Len Crowhurst

Bert Daniels

Bob Foreman

Mick Pearce

Dave Riley

Brian Simpson

Robert Smith (Nige)

Ralph Thompset

My apologies to any others who I may have omitted.

APPENDIX 2

Spring entry 1958 Fitter Apprentice Entry
(Advanced entry next door in ATC)

Mick Beer

Johnny Blezzard

Pete Brooks

Vinny Cottingham

Paul Gurney (Spike)

Bernard Hargan (Paddy)

Len Harris

Geoff. Hayward

Ernie Hockney

Mick Moad

Cyril Moffat

Bruce Naylor

'Spud' Taylor

Ron. Walters

Dave Wolf

John Workman (Stacy)

Dudley Young

Again, apologies to those I have forgotten.

APPENDIX 3

A balanced view

It must be understood that the dockyards were in many ways a type of insurance policy against a sudden urgent requirement to prepare and repair the Navy's warships and submarines. This meant that a 'captive' workforce of fully-trained and highly-skilled tradesmen and their associated requirements in terms of tools, workshops and materials had to be readily available.

Most of the dockyard workforce earned very low wages and relied on bonus payments and overtime to make a reasonable wage. This money was often earned in extremely poor working conditions, particularly on board the ships and submarines while they were under refit.

There was also a moral, if not mandatory, requirement by the Navy to employ war-damaged and other disadvantaged personnel.

Although the dockyard pay was poor, it gave its workforce the dignity of a regular wage, and a chance to improve themselves. The vast majority were conscientious, loyal and extremely hard working, some even to the detriment of their health, and they should be applauded for their efforts.

When a balanced view is taken, I can now see that the apprenticeship system was an invaluable stepping stone to a multitude of managerial, technical or scientific opportunities, if you made the effort and were interested and determined.

I now believe that there was a lot of truth in what my old dad (himself a 30+ years dockyard workman) used to say: 'The dockyard apprenticeship is the finest in the world, and if you stick to it, the world's your oyster.' I'm not sure the world was my oyster, and engineering fitting *per se* was never going to be my preferred long-term employment, but my apprenticeship left me with excellent skills and helped me to achieve most of my long-term career prospects and eventually a reasonable standard of living.

In common with the other Services, the dockyard was an excellent trainer. Apart from its own internal training centre covering management skills, scheduling, planning, effective speaking etc, a multitude of technical training was available. Establishments such as the DoE (Department of the Environment) training centre at Cardington taught plant engineering subjects, including air conditioning, boilers and electrical topics, while the naval establishments, mainly at Portsmouth, ran excellent courses by top-level trainers on in-service equipment.

A particularly good area was the weapons, where almost every equipment was covered by courses at HMS *Excellent*, *Vernon*, *Collingwood* or *Sultan*.

On reflection it is perhaps not surprising that this training was available and necessary for the dockyard workforce, as they were required to install, repair and maintain such diverse equipment, including:

Main engines, in various forms – steam, diesel, gas turbines and nuclear.

Auxiliaries: turbines, pumps, compressors, air conditioning and refrigeration.

Underwater fittings: propellers, shafts, rudders, bearings, valves, sonar, hydrophones and torpedo tubes.

Weapons: main and secondary systems.

Electrical and electronic: supplies, radar and radio.

Associated services: dockside cranes, pumps, lifts, transport, laundry and rope-making equipment, canteen equipment, etc.

With all those skills under our collective belts, we really were the unsung heroes. Weren't we?